Innovation in India

Also by Suseela Yesudian

INDIA: ACQUIRING ITS WAY TO A GLOBAL FOOTPRINT (edited, Palgrave Macmillan 2012)

Innovation in India

The Future of Offshoring

Edited by

Suseela Yesudian

Executive Director, Aditya Birla India Centre, London Business School, UK

palgrave
macmillan

First published 2012 by
PALGRAVE MACMILLAN

Palgrave Macmillan in the UK is an imprint of Macmillan Publishers Limited, registered in England, company number 785998, of Houndmills, Basingstoke, Hampshire RG21 6XS.

Palgrave Macmillan in the US is a division of St Martin's Press LLC, 175 Fifth Avenue, New York, NY 10010.

Palgrave Macmillan is the global academic imprint of the above companies and has companies and representatives throughout the world.

Palgrave® and Macmillan® are registered trademarks in the United States, the United Kingdom, Europe and other countries.

ISBN 978–0–230–30067–5

This book is printed on paper suitable for recycling and made from fully managed and sustained forest sources. Logging, pulping and manufacturing processes are expected to conform to the environmental regulations of the country of origin.

A catalogue record for this book is available from the British Library.

A catalog record for this book is available from the Library of Congress.

10 9 8 7 6 5 4 3 2 1
21 20 19 18 17 16 15 14 13 12

Printed and bound in Great Britain by
CPI Antony Rowe, Chippenham and Eastbourne

Contents

List of Tables and Figures

Tables

Figures

Notes on Contributors

K. Balakrishnan is Professor of Marketing at the SDM Institute for Management Development, Mysore, India. He researches contracting and corporate management.

Barnali Chaklader is Associate Professor of Finance at the Institute of Management Technology, Ghaziabad, India. She researches accounting and control, corporate finance and strategic cost management.

Rajat Gera is Associate Professor of Marketing Management at the Institute of Management Technology, Ghaziabad, India. He researches service quality and its consumer consequences, e-learning, sales force automation, innovation and technology, services marketing and product management.

Phanish Puranam is Professor of Strategy and Entrepreneurship and Co-Director of the Aditya Birla India Centre at London Business School. He is also Chair of the school's Ph.D. programme. He researches and consults on the design and management of strategic relationships between organisations. His first book, *India Inside* (2011), co-authored with Nirmalya Kumar, was published by Harvard Business Review Press.

Doris Rajakumari John is Professor of Marketing at Chennai Business School, Chennai, India. She has specialised in developing case studies as pedagogical tools for management education.

Ananthi Rajayya is Lecturer at the Albertian Institute of Management, Cochin, India.

Sathyanarayanan Ramachandran is Professor of Marketing at Chennai Business School, Chennai, India. He researches brand management, advertising and cross-cultural marketing.

Vrajlal K. Sapovadia is Professor of Finance and Accounting at IIM Indore, India. He researches business strategy, corporate governance and management accounting.

Foreword

To many readers, 'offshoring' and 'innovation' may seem like strange bedfellows. While India's success at becoming the world's hub for offshored services is now common knowledge, it remains less clear whether the country can make the transition from being the world's provider of fairly standardised knowledge work done to other's specifications, to becoming a genuine locus of innovation that has global impact. The challenges seem fairly obvious: distance from customers in the developed world, a surprisingly shallow pool of high-skilled talent and an Intellectual Property (IP) regime whose robustness is yet to be proven. On the other hand, the potential talent pool remains deeper than elsewhere in the world, and if the global delivery model (the workhorse of the IT and BPO offshoring industries) could be extended to higher-end innovation-related work, then talent in India could yet generate innovations for the world.

While the employment opportunities generated in an 'innovation as a service' sector must necessarily be smaller than those in commodity services, there are nonetheless several reasons why developing such a sector in India may be worthwhile. Greater value added, and therefore potentially greater profitability, may well generate large diffusion-of-wealth effects. There is also a potential incubation effect as individuals in the sector move on to become entrepreneurs. In some sense, building an export-oriented innovation ecology may prove to be an alternative to the existence of strong research-oriented universities as breeding grounds for innovators, and such an ecology would effectively be subsidised by global customers. Finally, an 'innovation as a service' sector is less likely (though not immune) to be a hostage to wage arbitrage opportunities that arise elsewhere in the world.

My own interest in the offshoring of services dates back at least to 2003 when I began investigating early attempts by Indian firms such as Dr Reddy's Labs and Biocon to replicate the success of the IT services industry in contract R&D in the life sciences sector. A talented doctoral student (and now a professor at the Indian School of Business), Kannan Srikanth, helped me learn about the global delivery model as an organisational innovation. In our academic papers, we have analysed how this model takes work that was formerly performed in one location and one firm, distributes this work across multiple firms and locations, and specifies the means to reintegrate the results.

In more recent work with Saikat Chaudhuri (Wharton), we have been exploring how the model transfers to R&D services. A parallel stream of research uses patented data to understand the nature and impact of innovation originating in India, and involves co-authors Tufool Al-Nuaimi (Imperial), Gerry George (Imperial) and Suma Athreye (Brunel). Some of this research is discussed in my book *India Inside* (Harvard Business Review Press, 2012) co-authored with Nirmalya Kumar, my colleague at London Business School and Co-Director of the Aditya Birla India Centre. The key point of the book is that products that are 'Made in India' are not the only form of innovation with global impact that India can produce; much innovation that may occur for global customers and consumers may be invisible to them unless Intel's approach to branding its microprocessor ('Intel Inside') were also to be applied to these Indian contributions – hence the title.

I am thus particularly pleased to see this edited volume, in which Dr Suseela Yesudian pulls together several cases that explore whether and how the services-offshoring sector in India is making the transition towards greater value added and innovative work. These cases were developed by academics in India as part of a case study project titled 'Innovation: The future of offshoring?' hosted at the Aditya Birla India Centre at the London Business School in 2009. The Centre was funded through the generosity of an alumnus, Mr Kumar Mangalam Birla, in memory of his father, one of India's pioneer globalisers. I have had the honour to serve as Co-Director of the Centre for several years now. One of the mandates of the Birla Centre is the development of case studies that showcase Indian business developments and enable these to be discussed in B-school classrooms around the world.

I congratulate the authors of the cases contained in this volume. Writing a case study using in-depth data from both secondary and primary (interview) sources is a time-consuming task, but if done well can result in a context for simulated problem solving by students, as well as a documented slice of business history that can be useful to the analyst or curious reader. Dr Yesudian has worked to weave together the various cases in this volume to ensure 'interoperability' – and I can assure the reader this is no mean task. It takes countless hours of editing, fact checking and synthesis, which result in a creative output that is not to be valued any less than any of the cases themselves. Indeed, if this collection of case studies means more to the reader than the sum of the parts, the credit is Dr Yesudian's.

Phanish Puranam
London 2012

Acknowledgements

A special thanks to Professors Phanish Puranam and Nirmalya Kumar. The research costs for this book were supported by the Aditya Birla India Centre at London Business School. The Centre and London Business School are grateful to Kumar Mangalam Birla for generously funding the Centre and supporting its work.

1
Symphony Services – Playing a Different Tune

K. Balakrishnan

The morning of 17 September 2009 dawned bright and sunny in Bangalore, a city widely regarded as India's Information Technology (IT) capital. Amitava (Amit) Roy, COO of the Indian operations of Symphony Services Corporation (Symphony), a provider of outsourced product development solutions in the software sector, was in his office poring over Zinnov's (a leading management consulting company) latest R&D Service Providers Rating. Alongside him was C. Mahalingam (known to all as 'Mali'), the chief people officer and head of human resources. Zinnov's report was indeed gratifying. This survey was conducted in 100 companies in India, China, Russia, the Ukraine, and Central and Eastern Europe (CEE), and Symphony Services emerged as the top-ranked player in its chosen vertical, software product development. Amit considered the result a vindication of the organisational structural changes he had initiated in 2007, which had enabled Symphony to respond faster and better to changing customer expectations. Nevertheless, Amit wondered whether he had done all that was required to position Symphony appropriately for the challenges ahead.

1.1 Company background

Founded in 2002 by Dr Romesh Wadhwani, the Symphony Technology Group (STG) was by 2008 a US$2.5 billion organisation that attempted to combine great companies with innovative first-to-market technologies and services with the objective of providing revenue growth to their customers. STG's mission was to invest in and operate excellent technology companies. STG actively engaged with each Group company, providing the financial backing, long-term commitment, operational support and strategic insight needed to achieve business performance and revenue growth through innovation.

Symphony Services was also founded in 2002. With over 150 clients and 39 per cent year-on-year growth, Symphony was ranked the number one Outsourced Product Development (OPD) Vendor in 2009 by *Global Services* magazine, included in the *Global Services* 100 list for the fourth consecutive year, named one of the top 100 innovative service providers in 2009 and recognised as the number one Software Engineering Services Provider and listed in the Top 50 Best Managed Companies by 'Black Book of Outsourcing'. Symphony expected to close FY2009 with revenues of US$280 million, with 90 per cent of its revenues originating from work in the company's Indian centres.

Symphony's clients include product companies such as AMD, Avaya, Autodesk, Hyperion, Juniper Networks, Motorola, Nokia, Oracle, Red Hat and Teradyne, and a whole host of service organisations. In 2009, Symphony operated out of Bangalore, Beijing, Boston, Dallas, London, Mumbai, Nashville, Palo Alto and Pune. The company had a delivery record of close to 1000 product releases in 2007 and 644 product releases in 2006. Compared to the 'most-effective' client centres whether onshore or offshore, Symphony has been able to demonstrate productivity enhancements ranging from 90 to 200 per cent. It has achieved Six Sigma process efficiency levels and Capability Maturity Model integration (CMMi) Level 4 process maturity rating. Table 1.1 shows the main players who operated in the same space as Symphony.

Table 1.1 Symphony's main competitors

Company	Annual Turnover (US$ million)
Persistent Systems	110
Global Logic	100
Ness (ITO + Product development)	540
Virtusa	160–80
Mindtree (Product development)	60–70
Wipro	700–900
HCL	800–1000

Source: Symphony.

Symphony's service range spans:

- Product Management: Symphony accepts end-to-end responsibility for the product management function, including obtaining wide-ranging customer feedback, market and competitive analysis, managing release cycles, prioritisation of point and major release functionality, and working with the client's product marketing teams. Symphony performed the product management function for 25 different products for clients by 2009.
- Architecture and Design Services: Symphony considers software product architecture and design as integral to its full product development life cycle (PDLC) capability.
- Product Development Engineering: Symphony's team of highly skilled software architects and engineers could take a product requirements document and develop the complete product.
- Testing: To improve test productivity and effectiveness Symphony has developed Symphony Test Engineering Management Suite (SympTEMS), a comprehensive and unique Symphony QA solution to support the 'Full Test Life Cycle'. The success of Symphony's approach is evidenced by the deep, long-standing relationships that they enjoy with their clients that include leading product companies and service organisations.
- Performance Scalability and Reliability Testing: PSR Testing at Symphony measures the current performance of the client's product and provides a health report, identifies gaps between current and expected performance to identify key problem areas and functionalities, and provides specific recommendations and performance improvement strategy to the design and implementation teams.
- New Service Identification and Development: Symphony helps unearth new revenue opportunities through the creation of new offerings such as tailored upgrades, pre-packaged customisations and fixed-price standardised migration which lead to accelerated rollouts of new licensed products.
- Transforming Professional Services Operations: One of the key innovations introduced by Symphony is to flip the traditional professional services paradigm, where today 80 per cent or more of the effort is made by costly on-site resources, with perhaps a small portion of the customisation or upgrade programming done

off-site. In the Symphony model most of the work is done off-site and, in fact, offshore.

Symphony's clients are on the whole satisfied with their vendor's efforts. Robert Gerston, chief development officer of Oracle Hyperion stated: 'We needed to increase our R&D capacity, tap into global talent pools, and realign our existing development skills, faster and more cost-effectively than the competition. Our collaborative multi-shoring approach with Symphony Services has enabled us to accomplish all this, and dramatically speed the time-to-market of our products.' Greg Nicastro, senior vice-president of product development, Iron Mountain, validated Symphony's accent on innovation: 'Other companies may have come to India for the cost advantage, but we're here for the innovation' (Symphony, 2009).

1.2 The global software development market

By 2009, global software development had become a mainstream weapon for business performance and competitive advantage. Over the previous decade, an increasing number of companies, particularly in technology and software development have been tapping into the best talent they could find offshore. The motivation to move processes offshore has moved beyond simple cost savings to become part of business strategy in the software industry. While cost advantages remain a critical factor in the decision to offshore, other drivers carry almost equal weight.

A survey conducted by the Software and Information Industry Association (SIIA) in 2009 revealed that growth strategy was an 'important' or 'critical' driver for 84 per cent of respondents. Figure 1.1 shows the other drivers considered important by companies for global development.

Of the companies surveyed, 62 per cent began their offshore initiatives less than three years prior to the survey, with 15 per cent starting these initiatives within the previous 12 months. The data attest to the recentness of the trend to offshoring. Even with limited experience in global software development, many of these companies had reached a steady state of productivity (44%) or were looking for ways to improve further upon the systems they already had in place

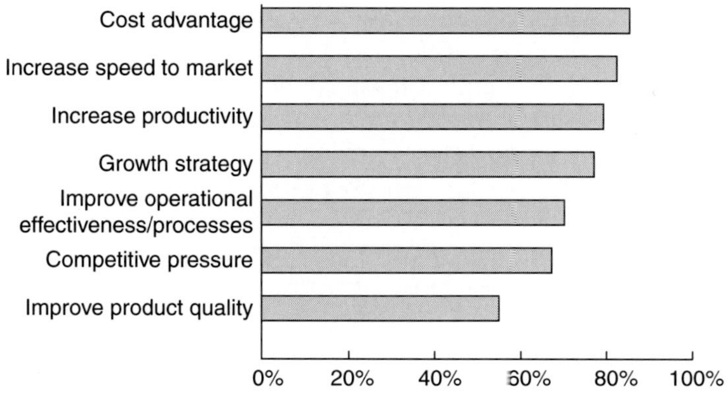

Figure 1.1 Drivers important for global development
Source: SIIA.

	Revenue (%)	Profits (%)
Negative	0	2
None	27	11
Low positive	27	32
Medium	26	23
Strongly positive	20	33

Figure 1.2 Impact of global software development on company financials
Source: SIIA.

(35%). Only 7 per cent were in a start-up phase and just 13 per cent reported they were struggling.

Not surprisingly, offshore R&D had a net positive impact on both the revenues and profitability of software companies. Of companies who worked offshore, 73 per cent reported a positive impact on the overall revenues and 88 per cent reported a positive impact on their profits (Figure 1.2).

There was no single model for offshore development among software companies. Half of those who used offshore sites/teams were working with an offshore provider, and one in three (31%) was working with a subsidiary or captive. In a significant number of instances (25%), companies were taking a hybrid approach that involved combining the use of outsourcing to an offshore provider while also operating a captive.

This represented a significant shift in how companies were accessing the offshore talent pool for their R&D organisations. In the early days of offshore product development, software companies had no other choice but to set up their own captive organisations. But the offshore landscape has matured and companies are more willing to work with an offshore provider. As a result, companies are increasingly willing to consider long-term contracts as opposed to short-term projects.

The immediate future of global offshore software development seemed bright from the survey of companies. Three out of four (74%) companies then not working offshore expected to initiate this activity in the future. The vast majority of those planning to go global intended to do so within 18 months. This intention to send software development offshore was in spite of the fact that three out of ten companies then not offshoring had undertaken offshore software development in the past. This meant that even some of those who had retreated from offshore initiatives in the past intended to return.

1.3 Projected industry evolution

Amit was concerned about how the market for R&D offshoring was expected to evolve in the near term. With the global economic meltdown of 2008 having impacted R&D offshoring, 2009 was expected to end on a hopeful note. In 2008, global R&D offshoring to emerging markets (India, China and CEE) was estimated at US$18.7 billion of which India's share was US$9.4 billion, China's US$7.7 billion and CEE's US$1.6 billion. Worldwide, MNC subsidiaries (or captives) accounted for 63.8 per cent of the total markets while independent service providers such as Symphony accounted for the balance 36.2 per cent. The outlook for 2009 was a market growth of 6–7 per cent.

The key challenges that R&D centres were struggling with seemed to be morphing into a new set of challenges. Familiar challenges (in order of importance) were controlling cost escalations, enabling faster ramp-up, controlling higher attrition rates, improving productivity and upgrading technical leadership. Near-term challenges were, however, seen as showcasing value growth and India-centre relevance, upgrading technical leadership, increasing innovation capabilities, having increased focus on productivity and addressing job relocation concerns among US peers.

The economic meltdown had lowered the cost pressures for most centres in India. Meanwhile the R&D ecosystem in India was expected to become one of the strongest in the world in the next ten years. Some key points that emerged were as under:

- MNC R&D centres were expected to operate in strategic independence or as global strategic partners.
- Most R&D service providers planned to make significant R&D investments and were developing capability from conceptualisation to manufacturing.
- Indian start-up ecosystem was expected to become very vibrant with companies with Intellectual Property (IP)-led revenue and billion-dollar turnovers.
- Indian educational institutions were increasingly taking the lead with courses on entrepreneurship and technology incubators.
- India would boast of the largest number of cities rated as preferred locations for technology talent.
- India would become one of the largest consuming economies of the world in absolute and purchasing power parity terms with the largest number of small and medium enterprises (SMEs).

MNC R&D centres were expected to grow in sophistication with multiple business models:

The expectations of global clients were changing. Service providers were increasingly expected to evolve as partners to help them reduce the cost of solutions and add further value. Amit thought that Symphony was better positioned (or, at least should have been) than most others to face this challenge.

Finally, service providers such as Symphony were also expected to transform themselves considerably. From a purely time-and-materials approach, increasing emphasis on true partnership leading to risk sharing was the way industry experts imagined the sector to evolve. Skills were expected to span the entire spectrum from conceptualisation to manufacturing with internal IP generation and go-to-market capabilities.

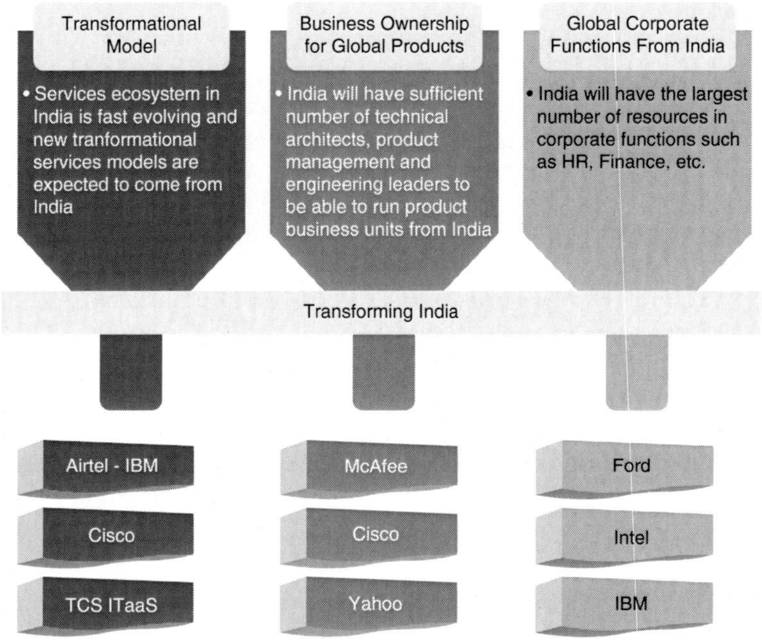

Figure 1.3 MNC business models
Source: Zinnov (June 2009).

1.4 Symphony organisational structure

Amit cast his mind back to the organisational structure he had inherited when he had joined Symphony and the subsequent changes he had effected. When Symphony commenced operations in 2002, its first set of clients – Siebel, Escalate Retail and Autodesk – were acquisitions courtesy of Dr Romesh Wadhwani. Symphony started with outsourced product development work for small companies where the initial thrust was maintenance of old products. Product development work on new products came later as buyer behaviour depended on whether the client was a start-up, small/medium or a large company and the triggers for outsourcing differed based on the size of the client.

R. Ramesh Kumar, senior vice-president in charge of enterprise applications, describes Symphony's initial approach in offering product development as a service as 'making a movie versus making a soap'. Symphony's original contracts were structured for the longer term but as new product development assignments were received it changed to a Build-Operate-Transfer (BOT) model. In the process Symphony developed deep domain knowledge in specific areas especially where it had set up global operating centres for large clients. The resulting evolutionary organisational structure is shown in Figure 1.4.

Amit was not one of the founding employees of Symphony; he had joined much later, after working at HCL. Dr Ajay Kela was the first COO and managing director of the Indian operations. Sometime after Amit joined, Dr Kela expressed a desire to leave corporate life and move on to other things. Amit had taken over from Dr Kela, who, he thought, had done a sterling job in building up Symphony from scratch. On taking over, Amit had not initially moved to restructure the organisation. But keeping in mind Symphony's mission to build a business around innovation and entrepreneurship, Amit felt that the existing structure no longer supported cross-discipline learning. A new matrix structure was put in place in 2009 (Figure 1.5). The new structure led to service line-led offerings in the fields of technology development, product quality, professional

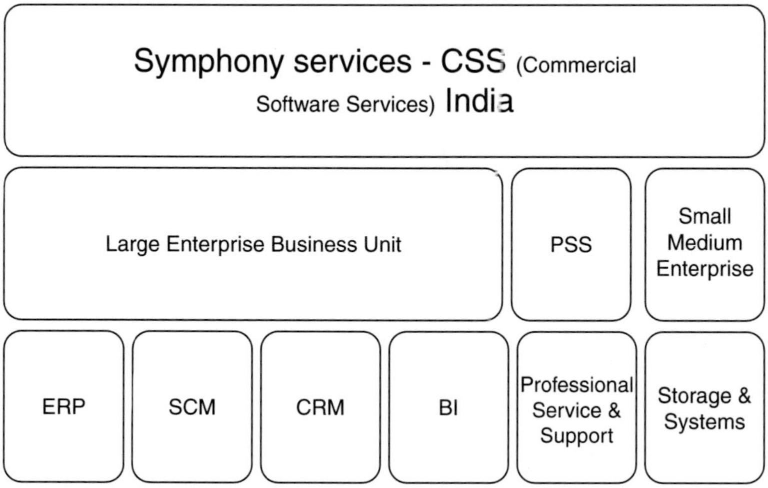

Figure 1.4 Symphony organisational structure in January 2007
Source: Symphony.

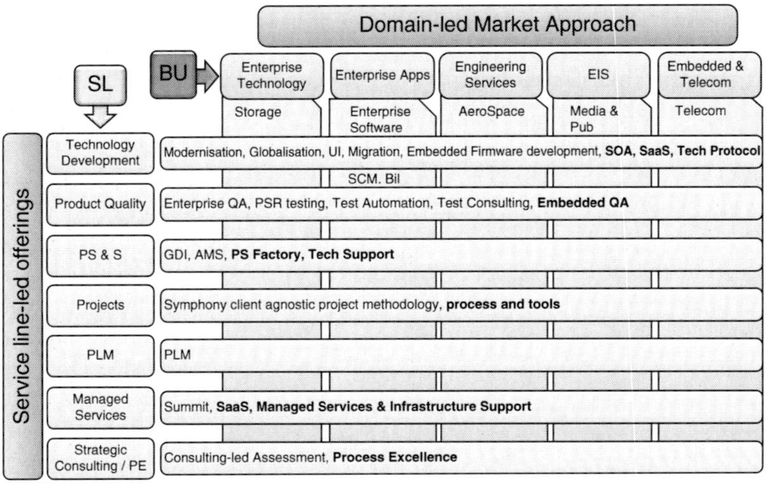

Figure 1.5 Symphony organisational structure in January 2009
Source: Symphony.

services and support, projects and product life-cycle management, and were made available to the customer through customer-facing vertical business units handling enterprise technology, enterprise applications, engineering services, enterprise information systems and embedded systems/telecom.

While Symphony was traditionally focussed on product development, the new structure also made it possible for the company to move into services as growth potentials emerged. Dr Romesh Wadhwani was initially unsure of the new structure, but Amit did have the support of Gordon Brooks, president and CEO of Symphony Worldwide. The success of the new structure was yet to be fully seen, but initial assessments were positive and the new arrangement seemed to be working.

Amit had his own ideas about how Symphony would evolve over the next five years. The offshoring market itself, he thought, would evolve like manufacturing. Cisco had already achieved 100 per cent outsourcing of hardware product development while as much as 50 per cent of its software product development was outsourced. Amit felt that the software industry thrived on the lack of standardisation but the increasing trend to outsource product development would lead to more and more levels of componentisation in terms of solution accelerators and canned process knowledge. The new organisational structure was expected to allow Symphony to proceed faster along the path of innovation and componentisation.

1.5 The Symphony innovation engine

By mid-2009, 63 per cent of Symphony's customers not only viewed it as an innovator but 42 per cent recognised the positive impact of Symphony's innovation prowess on their own business results. Two patents were filed with Symphony as the beneficiary, while as many as 33 were filed on behalf of clients. Alok Kumar Singh, one of Symphony's earliest employees was put in charge as senior director of the enterprise-wide Symphony Innovation Program (SIP). The core objectives of SIP were to establish the virtuous circle of 'Ideation-Discovery-Rewards' and mine ideas across PDLC. Further SIP strived to sustain organisational engagement, while the driving guideline was to 'encourage ideation and reward results'. To operationalise, Symphony adopted the Theory of Inventive Problem Solving (TRIZ) methodology, the two main benefits of which were the enhancement of personal creative capabilities and the ability to professionally apply numerous tools (including software tools) to obtain repetitive, reliable creative results in everyday engineering procedures (Table 1.2).

Table 1.2 Symphony product and organisational innovation

Product Innovation defined as changes in:	**Organisational Innovation by identifying new:**
• Features (what it does)	• Services and delivery models
• Technology (what Symphony uses to build with)	• Technology transformations to excel in delivery
• Process (how Symphony builds it)	• Organisational designs and managerial approaches
• Abstraction (who Symphony can build it for)	• Markets that would offer greater price margins
• IP creation (what Symphony can own and sell)	

Source: Symphony.

In the TRIZ methodology, the four categories of innovation were defined as follows:

1. Task Related (incremental):
   - Small improvements in existing process or features.
   - Excellence in delivery, extraordinary effort, high productivity.
2. Visible Impact (self-initiative):
   - New functionality (new or simplified feature, improved performance, usability, testable or modular code, test automation) undertaken largely on self-initiative.
3. High Impact (orthogonal):
   - Major new product features including support for new platforms, verticals or technology paradigms.
   - Major enhancements in quality or productivity through process improvements.
4. Game Changing (disruptive):
   - Investment in new verticals and sunrise areas.
   - Innovation (IP) teams: need client buy-in and experienced leaders.
   - Major innovation in process or business model that benefits Symphony on a long-term basis.

The structure that was formed to encourage innovation had at its apex the Innovation Resource Centre (IRC) which attempts to establish a sustainable ideas pipeline at the Global Operating Centre/Business Unit (GOC/BU) level. IRC established a system of innovation rating points and an innovation scorecard both at the GOC/BU level and at the corporate management level. IRC is an integrated portal for idea harvesting, incubation and value enhancement and tracked idea implementation and IP creation.

The ideas pipeline is designed to encourage innovation at all stages of the PDLC and is depicted schematically in Figure 1.6. The Innovation Program Council (IPC) owns and drives the implementation of approved Symphony ideas. Integrated into the IRC channel, the IPC provides details on the ideas under implementation at Symphony with regular status updates. IPC also actively helps IRC collate the data on business impact through implementation of Symphony ideas for a given period.

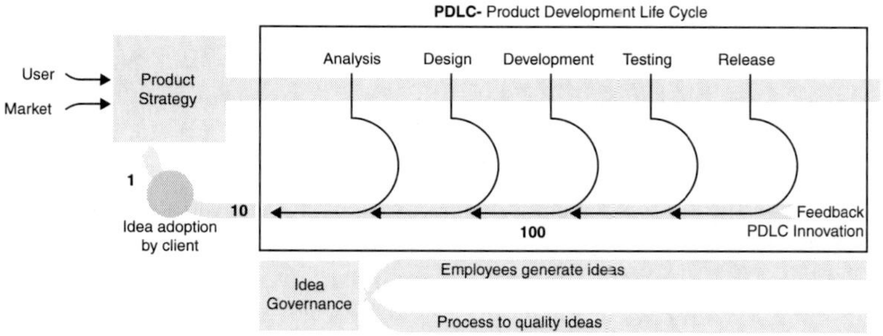

Figure 1.6 Symphony PDLC ideas pipeline
Source: Symphony.

The driving principle 'encourage ideation and reward results' has three programme phases:

- Educate: Define the programme and its benefits (August–December 2006).
- Engage: Deploy infrastructure and ecosystem to create the right culture for practising innovation (November 2006–April 2007 and continuing).
- Excel: Reap the rewards of the innovation programme through new revenues, delighted clients and engaged employees (April 2007 and ongoing).

The underlying philosophy to ensure that innovation is a sustainable process recognises that while the innovation programme could create the right culture, Symphony leaders need to drive and sustain it in their 'Circle of Excellence'. This requires a mindset change, one that necessitated maturity and conviction. It is emphasised that innovation does not occur through off-sites or 'ideas' day but needs to be embedded into the work culture. When the programme started, the focus was initially on internal objectives that would create a culture that encouraged and rewarded innovation, discover innovations that were already happening, operationalise the process of converting ideas to practical innovations and increase client delight by providing visibility into innovations being made. However, now that the process is more mature, the emphasis has shifted to structure future contracts to get more revenue for innovations, derive more revenue from existing clients for innovations, package and present innovations to prospects and connect and leverage external expertise.

The Innovation Council (IC) consists of around ten members and is the parent body, tasked with defining programmes, setting policies, creating infrastructure and monitoring implementation, and it ensures normalisation in how Innovation Rating Points (IRPs) are awarded. One hundred and sixty Innovation Mentors (IMs) are embedded in GOCs/Practice Lines/CoEs and support groups (1:20 ratio). They form the heart of SIP. IMs are champions of nurturing innovation in GOCs through promoting ideation, ensuring discovery and rewards, and mentoring and supporting employees on implementation.

The Innovation Program Monitoring Office (PMO) is an interface between IC and IMs to enable innovation progress and drive from top-down. PMO is also a driver of cross-pollination across the global operating centres, and connects IPC and Service Lines/Practice Lines/Centres of Excellence (SL/PL/COEs) to implement the approved ideas.

At the heart of the rewards programme is the system of IRPs and Table 1.3 shows the ratings scheme for innovations as defined internally by Symphony. Extra IRPs are provided for patents (granted and filed), published papers (internal and external) at Symphony, cross-functional ideas or Symphony-specific ideas, and for teams.

The awards for the best global operating centre and IM are based on innovation volume (total number of IRPs), innovation intensity (number of IRPs per engineer), innovation quality (percentage of ideas accepted by client and percentage of ideas that are high impact or game-changing) and innovation results (value creation through innovation). Table 1.4 summarises the overall results of SIP and analyses of approved client ideas and Symphony ideas.

1.6 Human resources at Symphony

For an organisation that from the beginning emphasises operating at the highest ends of the outsourcing/offshoring value chain, and does not consider IT-enabled services or system integration, the human resource challenge has been formidable. Recognising this, Dr Kela ensured that the HR function was adequately manned from the very outset when Mali joined as the chief people officer. As a product

Table 1.3 IRP scheme

Idea Complexity	**Scope**	**Accepted at Symphony?**	**Accepted by Client for implementation?**	**Implemented**
Task related (incremental)	Excellence in execution 'Good' design/ code/testing High productivity	0	+5	+5
Visible impact (self-initiative)	New or eliminated feature Major code restructuring Novel test approach	5	+10	+15
High impact (orthogonal)	High revenue/ profit impact New platform, database High client delight	20	–40	+60
Game-changing Pending (disruptive)	New product/ vertical idea New business model	20	+40	+60
Game-changing (disruptive)	New product/ vertical idea New business model	100	+100	+200

Source: Symphony.

company, Symphony needed to identify, recruit and retain engineers with the right mindset. The typical Indian BPO organisation is filled with engineers with a project-orientated approach. Engineers working on projects are typically used to clear start and end times with a complete disengagement on handing over and signing-off the completed project. They could then look forward to the next project, implying variety.

Table 1.4 Symphony Innovation Program results

	Results as on 31 August 2009
Total ideas submitted	6705
Total patents submitted	33 (filed for clients) 2 (granted for Symphony)
Total whitepapers submitted	140
Number of IMs	160
Number of ideas logged for Symphony	1233
Number of employees who participated	1688 (+IMs and IC), >54%
Ideas implemented	806
High impact ideas	329

Source: Symphony.

Those working on products need to become familiar with the business case, acquire deep domain (rather than technology) knowledge and be prepared for long-term engagements. There is less opportunity for foreign travel compared to those on projects. A different type of maturity was called for, and those wanting to work on products needed to be aware of not only what appealed to them, but also what did not. As Mali stated, 'We are looking for people who not only know where they want to go but also where they don't want to go.' Such levels of self-awareness came only after some years of working and so Mali decided quite early on that Symphony would not resort to campus recruitment.

HR has to be clear of the psychographic profile of those suited to a product company. With Symphony's client engagements being longer-term and linked to specific product lines, there is less need for significant bench strength. Where project companies and system integrators work with bench strength anywhere from 30 to 50 per cent of total employee strength, Symphony does not exceed 5 per cent. The recruitment challenge for HR is not only to qualify prospective employees but also to identify where they could be found. Fortunately for Mali, the numbers he needed are nowhere near that of an Infosys or a TCS.

Lower bench strength leads to a leaner and meaner organisation, but it also creates greater difficulties in convincing a new client account of their capabilities. Over time Symphony's technical and engineering prowess came to be recognised in the market, but a prospective new client was often in doubt of the bandwidth available. Project companies and system integrators were accustomed to showing the numbers on the bench when pitching for a specific account as evidence of their ability to ramp up to project requirements pretty fast. In many cases bench strength was the clinching factor for a client in a great hurry for an implementation of some enterprise-wide application.

For Symphony, however, engineering capabilities rather than bench strength is projected as the parameter of interest. Nevertheless it is quite difficult for a client to accept that work on an assignment would seriously commence only after engineers are identified and selected, and join Symphony and get briefed on requirements. HR here acts as a true strategic business partner; when Symphony Marketing presents its pitch to the customer, Mali would be present to showcase how Symphony has perfected the art of scaling up the necessary human resources in time for the assignment.

1.7 Conclusions

Amit was clear about the future focus areas for Symphony: Enterprise Applications (which include financial applications, retail, business intelligence, Customer Related Management or CRM and Enterprise Resource Planning or ERP); Enterprise Technologies (which include storage system management and security); Embedded applications (including telecom, medical electronics and health care); e-commerce and information service providers (who are portal based); and finally, Engineering Services (which include aerospace and automobile). With all this, Amit wanted to turn Symphony into a billion-dollar company in three years. 'Mali', asked Amit, waving the Zinnov report at him, 'Do you think our innovation programme and our ability to find manpower can really take us to that goal?'

2
Globalisation of Research and Development Centre: How GE does it in India

Barnali Chaklader

Ever since Abhijay Verma graduated from the Indian Institute of Technology (IIT), Madras in 1999, he has been in the US. A brilliant student, Abhijay was also an intelligent and hardworking scientist. He worked in a well-known research and development centre in New York as a scientist. His boss and MD, Steve, was quite happy with him and was even considering promoting him. Married to a north Indian lady for the past six years, Abhijay has a three-year-old daughter. He was often spoken about as a happily married man with a high-paying job. His work provided him with the freedom to concentrate on research and the centre's infrastructure was comparable to the best, and he didn't have to deal with administrative matters. His company's high-performance culture laid emphasis on high-integrity business practices, along with work–life balance. The 'yes boss' culture was almost non-existent. Everything seemed just fine for Abhijay but often he would look sadly out of the window and reminisce/wonder about his home country. Going back to India and settling down there was always on his agenda. The option was always there, but would he get the same kind of work environment that he had at his R&D centre in New York? Would he get a high-paying job there and an understanding boss like Steve? These were some of the questions that were going through his mind. He asked some of his IIT classmates to search for a research centre in India that would give him the kind of job satisfaction that he was getting in the US. One day he received a phone call from his scientist friend, Anshuman, in Bangalore (India), who informed him about GE's John F. Welch Technology Centre (JFWTC) in the city.

This is not only Abhijay's story. This is the story of many an ambitious Indian engineer and scientist working overseas, who have been drawn towards JFWTC with the intention of doing cutting-edge research back home in India.

2.1 Company background

In 1876, the same year as the Centennial Exposition in Philadelphia, Thomas Alva Edison opened a laboratory in Menlo Park, New Jersey, and from that laboratory came one of the greatest inventions of that time, the incandescent electric lamp (GE, 2009). The Edison General Electric Company was established in 1890 by bringing together various businesses. The Thomson-Houston Company, another electrical innovation company, also emerged during the same time, and became Edison's main competitor. As both companies grew, it became increasingly difficult for either company to rely solely on their own patents and technologies and produce complete electrical installations, and so in 1892 the two companies merged to form the General Electric Company (GE). GE's businesses, such as lighting, transportation, industrial products, power transmission and medical equipment, were all part of Edison's initial enterprise and are still part of GE today. The first GE Appliances electric fans were produced in the early 1890s, and a complete range of heating and cooking devices were developed in 1907. In 1917, when the US government began its search for a company to develop the first airplane engine 'booster' for the fledgling US aviation industry, GE Aircraft Engines was formed, but the term only came into use in 1987. In 1930 the first GE Plastics department was created, a direct result of Edison's experiments with plastic filaments for light bulbs in 1893 (GE, 2009).

GE's portfolio comprises a broad range of products and services: from jet engines to power generation, financial services to water processing and medical imaging to media content. GE is a global company and operates in over a 100 countries, with a total work force of around 300,000 people. The importance of hiring employees with local market knowledge is reflected in the fact that over half of GE's employees are located outside the United States.

2.2 John F. Welch Technology Centre

> As GE continues the push into new technology frontiers and provides world-class products and services to our customers, we need

> to look at research and development through a global prism. The opening of this Technology Centre marks a new level of commitment by GE in India.
>
> John F. Welch Jr, former GE Chairman and CEO

The John F. Welch Technology Centre (JFWTC) in Bangalore was set up in September 2000 and quickly became an integral part of GE's research and development capability in less than a decade. The centre carries out basic research but also develops products in such diverse areas as power generation, medical imaging, aircraft engines and financial services. To help accelerate the conglomerate's advanced technology delivery to its customers, JFWTC collaborates with three other global research centres in China, Germany and the US (Kulkarni, 2009).

GE invested close to US$175 million to create a lush 50-acre green site with several state-of-the-art technology labs dotted around the campus. The centre has buildings named after Martian probes, such as Galileo, Odyssey, Voyager, Pathfinder, Pioneer and Cassini. JFWTC employs more than 4000 scientists and engineers, and houses many R&D and engineering labs focused on areas such as mechanical engineering, electronics and electrical system technology, ceramics and metallurgy, polymer science and new synthetic materials, to name a few. JFWTC has become the global hub of technology and innovation for GE and more than 950 patents have been filed from the centre. Outside the US, it is the largest R&D centre working on technologies that spans most of GE's businesses. This is the first and largest research centre outside the US and the brainchild of Jack (John) Welch, former GE Chairman, who conceptualised the idea of GE having a global presence. In 1982, 80 per cent of GE's revenue was from the US and 20 per cent from the rest of the world. A visionary himself, the former Chairman understood the potential of the huge markets outside the US and believed that in order to cater to these markets he should establish research centres there. He projected that markets outside of the US would grow to 80 per cent and that GE would not remain a US-only company. For this, globalisation and the need to cater to local markets had to go hand in hand. Part of the strategy was to hire employees from the local talent pool in markets where GE had a presence. The former Chairman believed that GE, a global company, should 'think global' and 'act local' since the customers, talent and revenue were local.

GE had planned to leverage Indian talent through the JFWTC and so further boost the company's strength in innovation and R&D. The then managing director of JFWTC, Guillermo Wille, acknowledged that the centre had grown to be one of the more important R&D centres for the company. It started with a big idea and it was always the intention to make it big, since GE believed in the intellectual capital of India. Of the more than 34,000 GE technologists worldwide, more than 5000 are based out of the three centres in India: Bangalore, Hyderabad and Mumbai. JFWTC is GE's first R&D centre outside the US and is now its largest integrated multidisciplinary R&D centre.

2.3 The R&D sector in India: An overview

The attraction of carrying out R&D in India and in its emerging high-technology industrial clusters was increased by factors such as the growing availability of innovative, entrepreneurial, scientific and engineering skills and manpower at competitive costs; ongoing globalisation of manufacturing processes and service delivery; and finally substantial and fast-growing markets. Cities like Bangalore, Delhi, Mumbai, Pune, Hyderabad and Chennai have so far been the preferred destinations for R&D in India. Factors such as the combined presence of foreign companies, research labs and educational institutes have made these locations attractive centres for R&D operations (Mitra, 2007).

US companies were designing everything from auto parts to consumer electronics in India through outsourcing or setting up their own facilities in areas such as Bangalore, popularly known as India's Silicon Valley. All these efforts and more represented just the beginning of advanced research and development in India (Knowledge@Wharton, 2005). Gone were the days when international companies retained R&D jobs at home and sent low-level work overseas. The trend had begun to move innovation and design work offshore, especially to India. More than 100 *Fortune 500* companies, including Delphi, Eli Lilly, GE, Hewlett-Packard and DaimlerChrysler, set up R&D facilities in India over the past few years. An Ernst & Young study identified India as one of the most favoured destinations for collaborative R&D, bioinformatics, contract research and manufacturing, and clinical research as a result of growing compliance with internationally harmonised standards such as Good Laboratory

Practices (GLP), current Good Manufacturing Practices (cGMP) and Good Clinical Practices (GCP) (India Brand Equity Foundation, 2005).

2.4 Innovation at JFWTC

GE's research institutions are cost centres, spending 2.5 per cent of GE's annual revenue, which is around US$4 billion annually (Ganguly, 2007). Yet the demand for high-end work is great and businesses are willing to allocate funds for innovation. For example, take washing machines: by reducing the rinsing process and adopting new features, JFWTC helped develop washing machines in 2004 that required only 10 gallons of water as compared to the usual 23 gallons. By breaking the rinsing cycle into four stages and introducing a nozzle to spray water from above onto the clothes, the technology team at JFWTC's advanced mechanical engineering unit was able to save water used for rinsing.

Innovation is driven by the need to find solutions to problems. So when the residents of a small town in Texas complained about the noise caused by a nearby wind farm of around 100 windmills, GE looked to engineers thousands of miles away at JFWTC in Bangalore (Sachitanand, 2008a). Engineers at the centre worked on the problem for months and were able to reduce the noise generated by the wing tips from a deafening 85 decibels to a more manageable 80 decibels. While the reduction appeared small – just 5 decibels – many experts agreed that it was huge leap in terms of wind power technology. Breakthrough innovation like this one is not new at JFWTC. The centre's engineers are at the forefront of technological innovation for all of GE's business units, and high-end work is increasingly sent to Bangalore (Table 2.1).

Mano Manoharan, the general manager of operations at JFWTC, noted: 'Innovation in India is not different from innovation at the other centres of GE. Innovating and designing large complex products or next generation products purely adds to the competitive advantage of GE.' Employees at JFWTC have a passion for innovation and often spend much time thinking about GE's next product. The goal is to ensure that their innovations are unmatched, difficult to replicate, and that the final product would command a good market share.

Research conducted at JFWTC could be short, medium or long term. RTS (ready-to-serve) projects constitute 10 per cent of the R&D programmes undertaken at the centre. RTS projects are short-term projects with an immediate impact. The bulk of the work (around 70 per cent) revolves around multi-generation product plans (MGPPs) that typically impact business in one to three years. The balance 20 per cent are advanced technology programmes (ATP) which are five to ten year projects that would change the game for a business, or create a whole new market, if they come to fruition (*The Economic Times*, 2003).

At GE, long-term projects are broken down into milestone short-term objectives, so that the objective does not remain the same throughout the period of a long-term project. There are various deliverables that keep people engaged. On completing one short-term objective, scientists move on to the next short-term objective. Using this technique, the long-term project does not get monotonous as objectives keep changing from one short-term milestone to another.

2.5 From globalisation to glocalisation

Initially GE brought products from the US to various markets outside the US. But slowly GE began to understand the needs of the local markets, and developed or modified products in its research centres and adapted them to the local markets. It then came to the stage where GE started developing products in its local markets and took them to the global markets. An example of such a product was the portable electrocardiogram (ECG) machine that was developed in India at JFWTC and exported to other markets. The portable ECG machine was the result of market-driven innovation. The machine developed was convenient, user friendly, cost competitive and easily available. GE proactively assessed market requirements rather than waiting for customer feedback. It also understood that products made in India were not just for consumption in India.

GE's new phase of globalisation is termed 'connected, scalable, localization' (CSL). The CSL approach has three simple principles at its core. Firstly, the 'connected' part of the strategy recognises that GE's competitive advantage resides in connecting and leveraging its technological and manufacturing excellence. Secondly, to be 'localised' requires developing products in and for emerging markets – an essential way to reach new customers. Finally, to be 'scalable' GE has to identify potential opportunities to take those locally innovated products to other emerging markets and also promote them in the developed world (Govindarajan, 2009). Therefore, GE develops a product which can be used in similar markets and vice versa. Before selling a product in a market they become local to the extent that they become part of the market. They feel the pulse of the customers. This strategy of GE, known as reverse innovation, is not an option but is important to compete in localised markets. In this way, GE is able to sell quality products in local markets at a competitive price. The adaptation of global products to local needs is termed 'glocalisation'. As Alok Nanda, the leader for thermal systems and gas turbine engineering stated, 'The phase that GE is in now has gone beyond globalisation and is referred to as glocalisation because one has to understand the local market needs and cater to that. Wherever the market is similar, the products can be sold.'

2.6 Product development

GE has been extremely successful in reducing its product cycle and as Guillermo Wille, the MD of JFWTC, noted, 'Brilliant scientists have shrunk the product development cycle in almost every business area that GE is in' (Ganguly, 2007). Reduction of the product development cycle was made possible because of the operational excellence and tools developed by engineers at the centre. The crux lay in innovation of not only products and technology but also the processes. An example of reduction in the product development cycle was the reduction of the design cycle of the jet engine from ten to 12 years down to eight to ten years. Several models are built and tested using sophisticated engineering tools and software before the actual final prototype is made and tested physically. The prototypes undergo many changes and fine-tuning before the actual engine is built. In that way, the number of product cycles that they prototype is reduced. Wille acknowledged the innovative work being done at JFWTC, as he observed, 'I have watched people come up with ideas, which they've pushed against all odds until they become viable products. It's the most exciting thing to work here' (Ganguly, 2007).

JFWTC has prided itself on being a forward-thinking organisation. They assess market needs and create designs for developing products that may only come into production and be marketable in maybe another seven to ten years. The challenge they often face is the non-availability of a comparable benchmark. Tools and techniques like the Design for Six Sigma (DFSS) process are helpful. DFSS, a quality-focused approach to design engineering, is corporate R&D's primary Six Sigma Quality initiative. With R&D leadership, DFSS is fast becoming engrained in company operations and is beginning to reap huge payoffs by way of high-spec products and services that meet customer expectations. Since there is no benchmark available, JFWTC takes feedback from their customers, sets their goals, devises a strategy and proceeds ahead. Being a quality-conscious company, GE has well laid-out processes in their manufacturing facilities, as well as quality control procedures for their suppliers. Thanks to the DFSS approach, quality is built into the products. They periodically study the processes adapted by their manufacturing units and suppliers.

The process of conceptualisation means that GE needs to look 20 years ahead and work on technology that will help them remain competitive in the long and short term. While planning annually for the next three years, they still need to keep in mind what the market will need in the next 15 years. Scenario planning is conducted, strategies are devised and the plan is conceptualised for the next three years. The company organises annual session-T (technology) that is led by the global research leader. Here technology leaders along with business programme managers talk about the needs of the markets and customers, and look at what technologies need to be developed or which technology is currently available that could help address the unmet needs of the market. There are several tool gates that helped ensure risk was minimised while the impact to the business is maximised. Any new technology developed is taken through a process of new technology introduction (NTI) with clear business deliverables.

Not all programmes are driven by the current business interests of GE. About 70 per cent of R&D have immediate short-term business impact, while about 30 per cent is work related to advanced technology – those that may not find an immediate need but could in the future. It is critical that any technology developed has to have business impact. Technology ready to be commercialised is taken through the New Product Introduction (NPI) process. After studying the markets and customer needs, designs are first conceptualised and then detailed designs are produced before the product could be manufactured finally. Some products are retired over time whereas certain products like gas turbines have a life-extension programme. Using advanced diagnostic tools engineers are able to extend the life of such products close to the end of their life cycle.

2.7 IP process and culture

JFWTC has filed more than 950 patents since its inception in 2000, thanks to a robust intellectual property (IP) culture and process. IP-related issues are worked on by a team of 80 engineers, 15 of whom were dedicated to training and educating employees on compliance and making sure that employees adhere to IP-related laws and regulations. In an interview Gopichand Katragadda, the general manager of operations at JFWTC, explained the various processes set up by GE for protecting IP and how they are reviewed regularly (Jayashankar, 2007). Every employee is educated on what constitutes IP and how GE safeguards vital information. The tone for compliance is set right from the start at the interview process. When prospective employees come for an interview, they are told directly about not disclosing any confidential information related to their work; they could only share what was already in the public domain. This prepares employees from a very early stage, and once they join GE they understand that the company is serious about IP protection and compliance. Employees are frequently trained and educated on how to comply with these processes.

GE has a mechanism for distinguishing between what is a person's previous expertise and knowledge, and the work done at the company. It starts by looking at where an idea is generated. Knowledge is not IP. At the time of joining, every employee is given a Blue Book (Jayashankar, 2007). As soon as they have an idea it is entered into the book and concurrently acknowledged by another manager with a time stamp. This left very little room for doubts or questions later on. The employee continues to keep a record of all further work related to the initial idea in the Blue Book until it gets to a stage where the idea could be patented. This is followed by a strict eDisclosure process where the idea is checked for originality and potentiality before being approved by a team of business and technology leaders. When an employee leaves the company the Blue Book has to be handed over to GE. The policy is clear: whatever ideas or discoveries are made during an employee's time at the company is GE's property. The authors of the patent are individuals but ownership of the invention remains with the company. There are legal ways for a person to continue working on a technology even after they have left the company. Patents could be bought or leased by another company, and so a new employer could license a patent from the individual's previous employer (Jayashankar, 2007).

2.8 HR: Recruitment, retention and development

According to Rajagopalan (Raj) Raghavan, the human resources leader of JFWTC, GE's vision for the HR function is to 'build talent, culture and capability for global growth' (Rangela, 2009). JFWTC has a rigorous recruitment process to meet the numbers and maintain the quality of talent required at the centre. Hiring takes place not only in India but also from outside the country. Over 20 per cent of engineers working at the centre have had some global experience, having either worked or studied abroad. These numbers give some indication of a reverse brain drain, and that GE is able to create jobs by offering employees the right culture and challenging work. The human resource function at JFWTC is considered a true business partnership, one in which it anticipates changes and maintains flexibility to ensure that research work is unaffected. The centre does not believe in poaching, and recruits people through advertising and job fairs: 35 per cent of the people are hired through employee referrals and 20–5 per cent through campus recruitment. Once hired, the centre ensures that new recruits are comfortable and have access to all the facilities from the first day of joining JFWTC. They would be welcomed by Raj or some senior member of the HR team, and everything is put in place so that they could begin work immediately without problems. JFWTC also recruits from universities within and outside India, and collaborates with many premier universities on their Masters and Ph.D. programmes. Thus the Centre ensures a two-way and long-term relationship with the universities, which helps them select graduates from these universities, an arrangement that benefits the university and the JFWTC.

For any technology company, technical depth and long-term experience is very important, and the HR team at JFWTC has in place systems and processes that helps to retain their talent. From creating a healthy work culture where fresh ideas are always welcome to providing over 200 technical and professional training programmes, and offering competitive benefits and work–life flexibility options, the HR team constantly benchmarks its practice to remain competitive.

GE supports employees who wish to pursue higher education. They noted that a significant number of people left the company to gain further qualifications. So a retention strategy was devised where GE would send employees on a sabbatical to do a Ph.D. or a post-doc on a research topic that was of interest to the employee and GE. Employees return after completing their studies and GE pays 80 per cent of their tuition fees and some living expenses. This was a win-win situation for the employee and GE.

Professional development is a significant part of JFWTC's HR strategy and the company invests heavily in employee training. Employees are trained on professional, soft and technical skills. Most of the programmes are developed at GE's global training centre in Crotonville, NY but some are developed locally. Employees have a technical career path where they could move from one level to another. Once an engineer is promoted to a Lead position, he or she receives a technology grant, which could range from a week's to several weeks' pay. This could be used to sponsor research or attend conferences and seminars. Tapping into the leadership trait of its employees is seen as an important part of the training and development programmes.

To recognise and acknowledge the work and contribution of their best technologists, JFWTC present the GE India Technology awards, the highest awards at the centre. The awards are named after renowned Indian figures and include the JRD Tata award for Building Reputation, Dr Radhakrishnnan award for Mentoring and the Raman award for being a Young Innovator. It is a rigorous three-month process where leaders nominate employees from their respective teams and a committee decides on the winners. As part of the award, employees receive prize money, a plaque and have a conference room named after them for a year.

Corporate social responsibility (CSR) schemes are an important part of GE's agenda in India and employees are encouraged to get involved. There are around 900 employees who spend two to three hours a week to educate deprived children in the community, look after the aged, organise blood donation camps and run workshops on health and hygiene in the poorest areas.

2.9 Looking ahead

Guillermo Wille knew that the environment and green energy was going to be an important area for them. They were already working on alternative sources of power generation and efficient distribution, and had developed an engine at JFWTC which they were testing with alternative fuels such as palm oil and Jatropha. He knew that JFWTC had a strong global brand image that spoke of an excellent work culture and fair compensation practices and could attract the best engineers and technicians. He considered whether it would be beneficial for him to set up one more centre in India or whether they should expand JFWTC. Wille and his team were finding strategic and innovative solutions that focused on harnessing the power of Generation Y by developing, deploying and connecting with them. Wille may have been worrying about a whole range of strategic issues but Abhijay Verma was convinced of returning to India and joining GE JFWTC in Bangalore.

3

Quatrro BPO Solutions: Developing Outsourcing Solutions Innovatively

Rajat Gera

Srinivas Pingali, executive vice-president of new product development for Quatrro, and former head of Accenture India's insurance vertical, considered the challenges facing the company in its quest to become a leading knowledge process outsourcing firm. Though the company had grown 300 per cent in the past year to achieve a turnover of US$70 million in 2008, it had projected its revenue at US$160 million in 2012 at a compound annual growth rate (CAGR) of 92 per cent.

Quatrro is a global services company offering business and knowledge processing services to organisations seeking higher operational effectiveness, greater flexibility and lower operating costs. It is a fourth generation Business Process Outsourcing (BPO)/Knowledge Process Outsourcing (KPO) firm with seven complementary business lines, each one focused on serving the needs of its target clients with technology-based expert knowledge services while leveraging the overall resources of Quatrro: operational excellence, global infrastructure and capital. With over 200 clients around the world, its leadership team, and in particular its founder Raman Roy, are considered the pioneers of the Indian BPO industry. Quatrro is Roy's fourth venture and second entrepreneurial adventure to provide innovative and creative solutions to markets not served by current BPO service providers.

Pingali's office, on the fourth floor in Udyog Vihar, 30 kilometres from New Delhi, is located at the centre of the emerging industrial hub and mega-polis of Gurgaon, which epitomises India's emergence as a global services provider since 20 years. Pingali has been associated with Roy for over 16 years and is closely associated with the company's strategic initiatives. He and Alok Narain, vice-president of employee development, discuss the strategic and operational issues related to the growth of Quatrro.

3.1 Indian IT-enabled services (ITES) industry

Outsourcing is generally defined as the contracting out of some corporate tasks to an external entity or person. And offshoring is the procurement of goods or services produced domestically by a company, from abroad, either from a fully owned subsidiary ('captive') or a third-party vendor. Outsourcing answers a company's boundary question: 'Do we perform an activity within the company or hand it over to someone else?' And offshoring answers the geographical boundary question: 'Do we locate an activity within the home country or abroad?' The drivers of outsourcing and offshoring are cost reduction, leveraging talent outside the company (or country), greater focus on core activities and accessing foreign markets. BPO is the movement of business processes from inside the organisation to external service providers (Click & Duening, 2005). According to the Gartner Group, BPO is the delegation of a business process to an external service provider who owned, administered and managed it, according to a defined set of metrics. KPO is the outsourcing of 'high-end' or 'up the value chain' jobs or services, which are above the standard call centre-related services. KPO is seen as creating value for the client by providing solutions to high-end processes, and as a result 'entails the shifting from simple execution of 'standardised processes' to carrying out processes that demand advanced analytical and technical skills as well as decisive judgment' (Evalueserve, 2004). For example, in the insurance industry simple processes like claims processing and customer support, which constitute the lower end of the value chain, could be outsourced to a typical BPO with process expertise, but outsourcing high-end processes like underwriting or asset management would require domain or business expertise and also analytical skills (Evalueserve, 2004).

The global market for business process services was expected to be US$172 billion by 2009 with about a quarter of these services being offshored. The compounded annual growth rate of the offshore component of business services was projected to be higher at 56 per cent compared to the overall growth rate of 8 per cent. While

India was projected to maintain a leadership position, its market share would decline (a slightly slower growth rate of 52 per cent), reflecting growth in other locations. Offshore IT and BPO industry was projected to grow to US$110 billion by 2010 (NASSCOM-McKinsey, 2005), while Indian exports of services was estimated to be US$40.8 billion in 2007 (NASSCOM, 2008) and was expected to grow at over 35 per cent annually. India was referred to as the global KPO hub and was predicted to corner almost 70 per cent of the US$25 billion global KPO market by 2010 at a compounded annual growth rate of close to 50 per cent (Evalueserve, 2004). Lower costs were expected to drive this growth, and the cost structure for a client was expected to be reduced by 40–70 per cent as a result of knowledge outsourcing (Evalueserve, 2004; Khanna, 2006). For example, in legal processes, offshoring even a fraction of the patent-drafting process could result in a 50 per cent reduction in costs (Evalueserve, 2004).

India was the preferred destination for outsourced services, and was well positioned for a number of reasons, including a relatively high educated work force, foreign investment-friendly government policies, a stable political climate and English language proficiency. India has steadily grown in its delivery capacity, higher-value capabilities and reputation in the last 20 years and is expected to continue its dominance in the sector in the near future. However, offshoring has evolved into a global service delivery structure, with China, Southeast Asia, Central and Eastern Europe and Latin America emerging as attractive destinations. Further the basic 'cost-effective' model of Indian outsourcing sector is likely to become unsustainable as wages rose annually by 10–20 per cent and average revenues declines due to competitive pressures.

The 2007 NASSCOM-BCG Innovation Report categorised the evolution of the Indian IT-ITES industry into three distinct phases. Phase 1 was an export-led growth driven by factor arbitrage for relatively commoditised services like application development and management with very little R&D investment. During Phase 2, the Indian IT-ITES firms gained domain experience and developed a reputation for superior delivery thus capturing value in the market. During Phase 3, firms were moving into higher value services like IT consulting, systems integration, engineering services and contract R&D. In the BPO space, end-to-end outsourcing services with multiple-year contracts had started replacing the wage arbitrage-driven transaction services.

The Indian BPO industry is thus at a point of inflection where future growth would be driven by innovation. According to Suchitra Narayan, IDC's (a global market intelligence firm) senior research manager for Asia-Pacific IT services, the BPO market in the Asia-Pacific region excluding Japan (APEJ) is expected to grow at a five-year CAGR of 11.2 per cent from US$17 billion in 2008 to US$29 billion in 2013, and platform BPO's would drive this growth (Narayan, 2009). Platform BPO refers to business processing services based on a vertical or horizontal technology platform.

'The value-add brought by platform BPO such as standardisation, scalability, economies of scale and pay-as-you-use functionalities are areas that fit well in the CFO's agenda in today's market,' explained Narayan, adding, 'We are seeing an increasing demand for BPO vendors that are able to go the extra mile and transform businesses as well as contribute to growth as opposed to traditional models.' Narayan suggests that BPO is no longer viewed as a mere cost arbitrage tool but as a potentially strategic transformational service.

3.2 Company background

Quatrro BPO solutions was created in 2006 by Raman Roy who was inspired to create something 'beyond the existing' with the business philosophy of 'creating value by innovation'. Quatrro operates in the BPO and KPO space, and focuses on high-end BPO services with a mix of incubation- and acquisition-led strategies targeted at the underserved/unserved markets. In a short time span, Quatrro has managed to establish itself as a BPO company headquartered in India, with multiple fulfilment locations, providing solutions to clients across the globe. The company has pioneered new high-value service lines and business models, and rendered a wide range of vertical and horizontal services to its North American, European and Asian clients. By December 2008, Quatrro employed 2500 people and its annual revenue was US$70 million (*The Economic Times*, 5 December 2008).

The company endeavoured to provide clients with business solutions through a combination of tools, platforms and business processes. The game plan was to extract top management teams from global corporations, incubate BPO companies in areas like mortgage, health care, legal services, market research, analytics and others, and later spin them off as independent companies. Quatrro was set up on a 120,000 square feet (double the size of Raman Roy's previous start-up, Spectramind) facility in Gurgaon, an upcoming high-tech cosmopolitan city located 30 kilometres from New Delhi. Roy initially identified 11 areas with the intention to eventually focus on five to six areas. Quatrro intended to become an umbrella organisation which would incubate multiple high-end BPO companies within its fold.

'Quatrro's "value by innovation strategy" involves attracting and supporting entrepreneurial management teams by building high-end third-party businesses in underserved and uncontested market spaces,' Roy explained, adding further that at the company, 'We have a string of pearls strategy. We will extract management teams from existing corporates and build high-end services delivery capabilities in virgin areas. We are in advanced stages of discussions to build our analytics and finance and accounts teams. Incubating companies is a critical component of the strategy' (*The Economic Times*, 6 June 2006).

3.3 Growth by acquisitions

Quatrro's growth strategy was a mix of organic and inorganic growth. It acquired companies which gave it access to a technology platform or an operations capability. In June 2006 Quatrro acquired the 300-people BPO arm of Flextronics (FSS BPO) which focused on the telecom vertical. In April 2007 it bought out Mauritius-based fund, eIndia's, stake in Chennai-based Scope e-Knowledge, a top-end KPO vendor with services spanning patent filing, knowledge extraction, legal processes and market research, with 500 employees comprising engineers, doctors, radiologists, MBAs and other professionals. Its delivery centre was in Chennai, India and it had offices in China, New York, Chicago, Orlando, London, Brussels and Cologne (Singh, 2007). In June 2007 it acquired the technology platforms' business operations and platform of USA-based Preferred Financial Group, Inc. to become the first BPO offering from an Indian company adopting the onsite–offsite model, the new business model being preferred by the software services industry in recent times. Quatrro acquired the technology platform and the origination business of the US partner to enable it to provide end-to-end fulfilment services to mortgage lenders across the US at a price-point projected to be 30–50 per cent lower than the prevailing processing costs in the United States (*The Economic Times*, 6 June 2006, 5 December 2008). In July 2008, along with hedge fund DE Shaw group, it acquired UK-based Babel Media, a provider of specialist outsourced services to gaming and interactive entertainment industry and games-focused localisation, certification, audio and print services across platforms through 500 employees in Brighton (UK), Los Angeles, Montreal and New Delhi (*The Economic Times*, 2 July 2008). In August 2008, Quatrro lined up US$250 million and teamed up with two foreign private equity firms to bid for three US-based BPO companies operating in niche areas, one of which was in the mortgage services domain.

Quatrro's operations spans both traditional BPO areas as well as newer areas and the company provides a range of vertical and horizontal service offerings in fraud and risk management services, mortgage solutions, technical solutions group, legal process outsourcing, finance and accounting, market research, knowledge and information search services, business support services, interactive entertainment and back office services, and gaming and testing.

It has a presence in the US, Sri Lanka, Singapore and China markets, where it offers services in verticals such as finance and accounting, health care, mortgage and banking, as well as newer areas in legal outsourcing, consumer analytics, risk management, clinical research and engineering design.

3.4 The promoter

Raman Roy is regarded as the pioneer of India's BPO and ITES industry. He is credited with setting up India's first offshore service centre for American Express and is instrumental in building the country's stature as the locale for remote processing, delivering world-class solutions and services. Roy started his entrepreneurial career with Spectramind eServices, one of the biggest success stories in the Indian BPO industry. He created more than 30,000 jobs collectively during his tenure at Spectramind, GECIS and American Express. In 2006, he tied up with the largest industrial conglomerate in Sri Lanka, John Keells Holdings, to develop the BPO business across Asia where his company Quatrro – formerly, Raman Roy and Associates – held a 22 per cent stake.

Roy was born into a wealthy Lahore-based businessman family who lost everything during the partition of India in 1947. With a degree in commerce from SRCC college of Delhi, he started working at VK Mehta & Co, a chartered accountancy firm, as an auditor and it was there that he learnt that 'auditing was not about the vouchers you are looking at but the process', and it was where 'he honed the process and felt that life is all about processes'. His varied career path meant that Roy wore many hats: as an auditor, consultant, business leader and an entrepreneur. He also lectured occasionally on outsourcing at Harvard, MIT and other institutions. On completion of his chartered accountancy exams, he received six job offers of which he accepted the one from AF Ferguson. In an interview with *The Economic Times*, Roy mentioned how he loved the culture at Ferguson and owed them a lot for all what it taught him. He was able to take all those lessons to all the subsequent places he worked, including Quatrro. 'That includes a culture of trust, competitiveness and professionalism' (Singh & Mukherjee, 2008). With a desire to make it big, Roy set up SRF Finance, the financial services arm of SRF, the third largest manufacturer of belting fibre in the world.

After setting up SRF Finance, Roy was invited by Tony Singh to join AmEx and was brought on board as CFO and head of technology of AmEx India. He said that 'the challenge got him hooked' (Singh & Mukherjee, 2008). Roy led the automation of the travel processes AmEx was doing in India, an achievement that was acknowledged when he was awarded the worldwide AmEx quality award in the US. He later helped the company launch AmEx cards too, this time as Chief Operating Officer (COO). He recounted, 'Looking back if that had not happened, BPO would not have happened in India! This job for the first time exposed me to the accounts reconciliation process for Amex' (Singh & Mukherjee, 2008).

Shortly afterwards, Roy left AmEx to join GE to start a call centre, a new concept and a challenge for Roy after dealing only with transaction processing at AmEx. In spite of doubts raised by GE boss, Jack Welch, and VSNL (the then Indian government-owned telecom services company) by emphasising job creation and foreign-exchange earnings via call centres in his presentation, he finally convinced VSNL to give him a chance. In 1998 GE gave him US$100,000 to prove that global call centres could work in India on the understanding that he would be fired if they didn't.

The first GE call centre, then called GECIS, had just 21 people, out of which 18 were VPs. The success of GECIS attracted big IT companies and he later started Spectramind eServices, his first entrepreneurial venture, which he later sold to Wipro in 2002 but which he continued to head till December 2005 (*Business Wire*, 2 September 2002). In January 2006, he started his fourth venture, Quatrro (meaning fourth in Latin; and the double R standing for his initials).

3.5 Service lines

Quatrro has seven service lines which are supported by horizontal process teams. The company differentiates itself by pioneering new high-value service lines in KPO/BPO areas, like risk and fraud management, knowledge and information research services, legal process outsourcing (LPO), interactive entertainment, and also by creating niche solutions for conventional BPO areas like finance and accounting, mortgage solutions and technical support. Some of the company's major acquisitions allowed it to enter into new service businesses. For example, Babel Media enabled it to rapidly enter the new area of outsourced services for entertainment. However, it also offers new services through incubation. Quatrro Business Support Services is a global outsourcer of specialised front and back office services in the areas of technical support and help desk, travel, telecom and health care verticals.

Commenting on Quatrro's growth strategy, Roy stated:

> Our model was not to incubate or acquire ... our model was to get into what we call uncontested spaces. Within those spaces we identified some areas that could be built organically, somewhere acquisitions were worthwhile and somewhere we would initiate the business organically and then do an acquisition. For instance, our mortgage and accounting businesses were both initiated organically and when we came to a particular stage, we did an acquisition. The spaces that we have chosen, the more established companies have not even entered. They may come in because they find it profitable, seeing what we are doing, but right now we play in uncontested marketplaces. There is no competition. Think about it. In gaming, nobody is in that space. We have 1,500

> customers, mid-market and small companies, for whom we do accounting and we use less than 600 people.
>
> Sengupta (2008)

A global sales force comprising domain and BPO experts provide sales and service support to a range of services to ensure prompt client and relationship management with clients across geographies. Quatrro's 13 production centres and offices are located worldwide: Chicago, Madison and Pleasant Prairie and Burlingame (US); Colombo (Sri Lanka); Montreal (Canada); London (UK); Pudong (China); Dubai; Singapore; and Delhi, Mumbai and Chennai in India.

3.6 The service product

Quatrro's main product can be termed as 'BPO Business Platform'. 'Platform BPO, is the bundling of technology, consulting and BPO, and helps synergistic value creation by delivering transformational value to clients using strategies such as global sourcing, technology innovation, process optimisation, scale and centralisation; it moves customers from capex to opex model,' explained Anantha Radhakrishnan, VP and head of business platforms at Infosys BPO (Kaur, 2008). Platform BPOs offer economies of scale and process standardisation and they allow vendors to de-linearise growth through large-scale productivity payoffs and pay-per-use revenue models, besides building their own IP. The vendor operates, maintains and takes care of upgrades freeing the client's resources. Since the model requires a blend of IT, BPO, analytics and domain knowledge, companies need to have in-house development capability and expertise in service delivery. Since platforms allow companies to address a much bigger market, they are especially attractive to small- and medium-sized companies who may not have had resources for having their own platforms. Roy noted, 'Quatrro was one of the pioneers in this segment and today we have customers on platforms. There is no other way for the industry but to accept platforms' (Kaur, 2008).

The platform-based model necessitated that customers trust their BPO provider to manage critical functions and handle confidential and sensitive information. It was the next generation in the development of the BPO industry from being the back office to being a trusted partner. 'BPO Platform requires high upfront investment in fixed costs and relatively low variable costs. It is the reverse of the traditional Indian BPO model and represents a totally different risk: reward equation for the industry. It is not a marginal, incremental activity as many Indian firms seem to suggest,' observed Akshaya Bhargava, CEO of the Butterfield Fulcrum Group (Kaur, 2008). The margins remain negative until the business got scale. Service providers need to offer full solution capability, that is, the technology has to be bundled with the operations and offered as a full solution so that the technology becomes irrelevant.

3.7 Quatrro's innovation model

Quatrro's innovation spans varied dimensions of business model innovation, business process design, marketing strategy, new product development and service delivery (Fig. 3.1).

Quatrro's mortgage processing solutions illustrates well the company's innovation in the sector since it transcended existing industry boundaries. The mortgage processing market meets the needs of mortgage banking institutions dealing with the challenges of rising interest rates, increasing instances of borrower default, shrinking origination, refinance volumes and competitive pressures. Mortgage BPOs manage processes across various parts of the mortgage

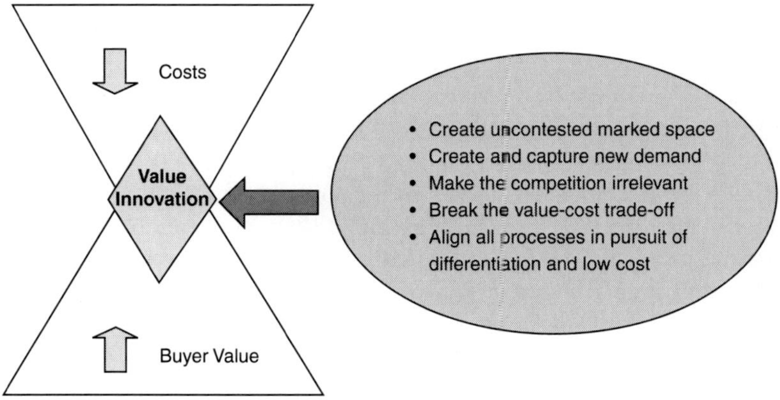

Figure 3.1 Quatrro model: Value innovation
Sources: Quatrro and Blue Ocean Strategy, W. Chan Kim & Renée Mauborgne (2005).

value chain, from origination and fulfilment to secondary marketing. Some vendors provide high-end services such as analytics and investor reporting. In 2008 the market for mortgage processing was estimated to be between US$6–7.4 billion while the existing BPOs' market size was approximately US$500 million. Analysts expected the outsourcing market to increase, as labour costs constituted a significant portion of the overall costs that mortgage banks incurred in servicing clients. Offshore outsourcing for mortgage BPO was expected to generate cost savings in the range of 30–50 per cent while customers experience cost savings ranging from 20–50 per cent over the life of the contract. The functions of a mortgage BPO can be clubbed under four distinct headers: new business acquisition, appraisal title checks, underwriting disbursement and servicing collections maintenance.

Quatrro does not compete in the existing space of servicing large banks in USA through outsourcing of non-core processes on an hourly payment basis, which is the industry standard. More than 70 per cent of the US mortgage market is controlled by large banks including Citibank, Bank of America, Wells Fargo and Chase Manhattan, which process 60,000–70,000 loans a month. Quatrro targets small- and medium-sized mortgage service providers, which processed approximately 100–1000 loans a month, and are seasonal players. Quatrro offers 'end to end' customised solutions, including the technology platform, which takes care of the complete process from origination to fulfilment. Thus, the client organisation could focus on its core business of marketing and customer acquisition without bothering about the scalability of the business. Quatrro also offers cost savings of up to 30–50 per cent while enhancing its own margins to the level of 30–40 per cent at scale, and looks at businesses with an annual turnover of around US$100,000–500,000, which constituted the long tail of the market. Quatrro allows small businesses to turnaround their cash flow at a faster pace without bothering about loan origination-related formalities which included document processing, regulatory approvals and customer verification. Their clients also benefit from direct cost savings. Quatrro could process the loan at a cost of less than US$500 per loan, while it normally took about US$1100 to do the same job in the US. This converts into revenues of US$35–40 per hour for Quatrro vis-a-vis US$10–12 which they would normally earn in the usual outsourcing business model. Thus, while the client is able to build and operate a highly scalable model which was also

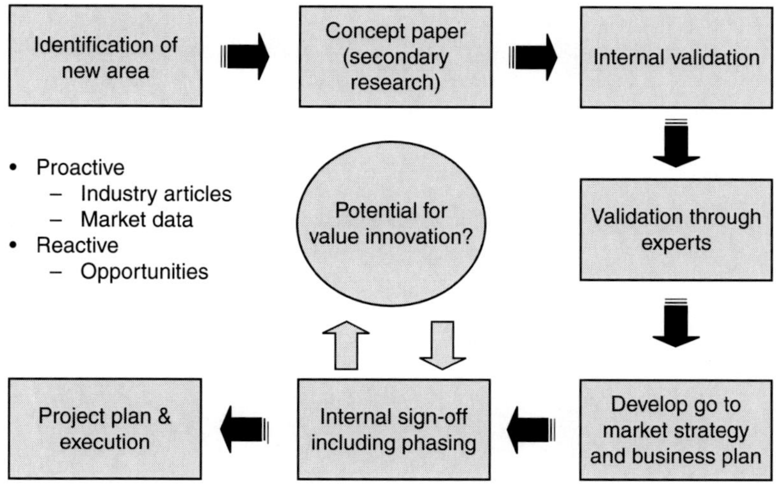

Figure 3.2 Quatrro's new product development process
Source: Quatrro.

efficient by 30–50 per cent, the BPO service provider earned three to four times higher margins above the industry average.

The service provider risk is reduced by only offering to outsource service processes which were transactional in nature. For example, the origination part of loan processing is largely standardised and involves very little risk to the mortgage originator who usually repackages it and parcels the servicing and management part of the loan to another company. Quatrro thus identified opportunities for new products where the risk was marginal or nil, and where customers were not being served by existing BPO service providers. The new product development process is shown in Figure 3.2.

3.8 New product development process

The new product development process follows a very structured approach (refer to Figure 3.2), similar to the stage gate model of new product development. However, it differs from the existing product development process as the opportunities identified are in uncontested market spaces where there is no existing competition and the customers are small and medium businesses. Thus an existing

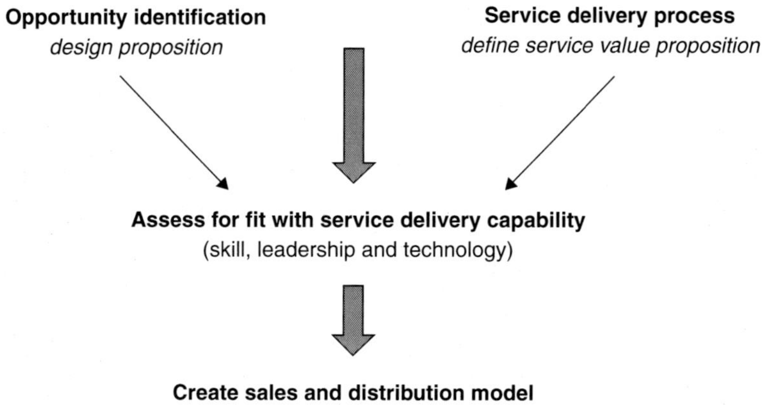

Figure 3.3 New service development model
Source: Quatrro.

business process was redesigned and offshored so that it could be delivered from a remote location using a technology platform. This required ensuring adequate fit between the new service process identified and the delivery capability of Quatrro. The company has adopted an onshore–offshore delivery model wherein professionals recruited by Quatrro are stationed at the client site while the process is delivered from India. The sales and distribution structure for each service vertical follows a hybrid model to reduce customer acquisition and management costs. The new service development process adopted is illustrated in Figure 3.3.

3.8.1 Opportunity identification

Quatrro searches for opportunities among non-customers. The WWH (Who-What-How) framework is used for identifying and evaluating opportunities. 'Who' (who within the product segment) answers the question of 'who should we focus on?' For example, while selecting the target segment for their mortgage products, the company follows a hierarchical model as follows. Banks in the US with mortgage services are segmented into large and small banks depending on the number of transactions per month. Since large banks are already served by the existing BPO service providers and has well-established processes, small banks are selected as target customers.

Further segmentation is done by dividing the small banks based on their ownership structure into community banks/co-operative banks/regional banks. Thus, the company identifies opportunities by focusing on the unserved or underserved part of the market where there is nil or negligible competition, and aims to create innovative service products which improves the business performance of the target customer.

The opportunity selected is further evaluated by answering the 'What' part of the WWH model using the RTS framework. The company tries to answer the question, 'if this is the target segment then what does it take to serve them?' The company follows a structured innovation model while evaluating the opportunities which would take into account the experience of the firm and its personnel, the ability to deliver the service, the platform which includes the technology aspects, whether a significant (70–80 per cent) part of the process is standardiseable, the nature of competition, and its domain expertise (leadership). For example, while deciding to offer platform-based origination products in the mortgage solutions space for small to medium businesses (SMBs), which are primarily small banks in the USA, the company discovered that the process was almost completely standardiseable; it had the requisite domain expertise and leadership and the technology platform (SAP based), and that existing competition was almost nil as there was only one competitor, which was a US-based company, and it was pricing its services quite high. The service product developed also enables the target customer to rejig its business model as it becomes flexible and scaleable, and allows the bank's management to focus on customer acquisition while relieving it of the burden of managing the mortgage-origination process and the capital expenditure on technology required for scaling up as the business grew.

3.8.2 Process development

The new service process development consists of mapping the existing process and disaggregating it into serviceable parts. For example, in the finance and accounting (F&A) vertical, the company had disaggregated the F&A process into standardised chunks, 'stock keeping units' (SKUs), a term used to denote each product unit in fast-moving consumer goods (FMCG) marketing. The client required some services on a regular basis which were packaged and sold through a monthly subscription fee which may be US$500 per month. These services in the F&A segment are among others such as accounts payable, accounts receivable, general ledger entries, payroll processing, all which are required on a regular basis. However, for intermittent services like taxation, the company offers a pay per use-based pricing option. Thus the platform product was packaged and marketed as an SKU while the customised component of the service was offered on a pay per use basis.

Thus, Quatrro leverages its domain knowledge by disaggregating client business processes into standardiseable and customised chunks wherein the business gains from the scalable part of its process by access to the latest practices and technology while freeing it to focus on the customer end of its business. At the same time, the company's non-standardiseable and intermittent processes are also taken care of on a pay-per-use basis. This enables the SMB to grow its business in an efficient and flexible manner. This also takes care of the people issues at the client end, as jobs are not eliminated since the business model is an onshore–offshore model. Quatrro employs professionals for the client – for example, a chief financial officer from the US – preferably one who could integrate the client's business process with the delivery model. The client thus migrates to an advanced technology (SAP or MS Great Plains based) which is scalable, and also gains from professional expertise provided by Quatrro. The standardised process becomes a platform product which is then marketed to other potential customers with similar needs.

Customer acquisition is driven by the reputation of the professional team which heads the service vertical. The mortgage service line is headed by Gary Bettin, who is the US head of mortgage business for Bank of America, and is a highly respected expert in the business. Quatrro acquires clients on the basis of its reputation, and industry experts who have 20 to 25 years domain experience and are leaders in their sphere. An exception to Quatrro's innovation engine is the service line of Legal Process Outsourcing (LPO), where the processes are highly situational and skill based, and therefore not amenable to standardisation. This creates some impediments to the growth of the company, an issue that Quatrro is keen to tackle.

3.8.3 Service operations

The service is delivered through a team of professionals hired from across the world. In an interview with KPO Consultants in 2009

Raman Roy claimed that 'Some of the largest RFPs of Quatrro are for risk management services. To deliver the same, we have recruited charted accountants, economists, MBAs and company secretaries along with lawyers in the area. Our risk management services are of a very high end job work of the data analysis of the Visa Card Management Services including investigations and other aspects applicable anywhere in the world.'

In order to assure quality and security in providing services to its customers, Quatrro has adopted Six Sigma, Kaizen and Lean principles which ensure elimination of inefficiencies and help create a continuous improvement culture. Quatrro has also embedded best practices from industry-relevant standards such as COPC Gold, ISO 9001, PCMM and SAS 70. It is an ISO 2001 certified company in terms of security standards and has also subscribed to a suite of information security standards. Quatrro is certified to ISO 27001; Data Protection Act, 1998, UK; and PCI DSS.

Given the sensitivity of its customers to information security, the company follows global best practices. In the same interview with KPOC in 2009, Roy emphasised the company's attention to security, 'We have CCTV, strict security in production departments and we track day to day activities of every person in the company. In this regards we have separated our "executive sitting area" from the production area. Our customers often make a visit to us to check the security standard of the company. They test the quality and security standard of the company through their regular visit[s] from time to time ... We are bound to do all that because it's a billion dollar business. We can't compromise with our quality and security standard.'

3.8.4 Growth issues

One of the biggest challenges that the company faces is scalability. Internal challenges include managing employee costs, which constitutes almost 60–70 per cent of the cost structure, and so the company has needed to ensure that the costs do not go up non-linearly while scaling up the model. This requires training of employees, enabling them to have requisite skills for multitasking so that they could serve the needs of multiple customers simultaneously. It also requires customisation of the technology platform so that the employee could work on multiple jobs without compromising the security of its clients' data. Another organisational issue which the company faces is developing the appropriate attitude of customer service among its employees who are highly qualified professionals serving the relatively less qualified proprietors and managers of small businesses, and who are more used to providing services to large clients who tend to have greater resources available to manage their outsourcing and offshoring initiatives. One of the biggest challenges for the company while scaling up its business model has been recruiting professionals with the requisite skills sets. While the company does not hire freshers who do not have domain experience, there is a need to develop new talent pools and ensure that they deliver the service with the appropriate attitude, for which the company conducts training sessions. Thus, while developing new products, the company needs to ensure the ability to deliver the service which is dependent on the availability of trained and experienced professionals with related expertise. The problem is not significant when the number of customers is small but as the customer base expands, creating a scalable organisational structure could be the biggest obstacle to the company's future growth.

3.8.5 Sales and distribution

The companies' go-to-market strategy is highly innovative and does not replicate the sales and distribution model currently adopted by the BPO service providers. For its first product Qresolve which targeted millions of personal computer (PC) owners across USA with remote troubleshooting (the first branded offshore service), Quatrro has adopted a multi-channel strategy which includes a portal (www.qresolve.com) and has partnered with one of the largest electronics distributors in the US, who markets and distributes its products (six monthly and yearly subscriptions) as prepaid cards which consumers could purchase off the shelf and even gift to others. For its mortgage and risk management service lines, it has developed a matrix sales structure with domain and product specialists. The model has been tweaked twice in the past three years and the company is planning to change it once again. The major challenge that the company faces is developing a cost-effective sales force structure which transcends the seven vertical service lines by offering appropriate domain-specific expertise while leveraging the customer base by cross selling. Developing a dedicated sales force for each domain increases the cost of customer acquisition while hiring generalists does not serve the purpose of acquiring customers based on domain-specific expertise of the company.

Quatrro could not fly its experts from the horizontals, especially from new product development, from India to the US to meet the customer for every specific issue which required expert knowledge as the size of the customer (mostly SMBs) in terms of sales turnover was not very high. This led the company to design an offshore–onshore service delivery model supported by a matrix go-to market structure wherein the three horizontals of BPO sales responsible for lead generation, channel sales and sales support provided sales support to the domain-specific sales professionals. The company had a domain-specific go-to market strategy wherein the channel structure for each service line was developed separately. However, the company preference was to distribute its services at minimum cost by leveraging the existing channel structure in the US. For example, for the distribution of its product Qserve, it tied up with two of the largest store chains which controlled almost 70 per cent of the distribution of electronic products in the US. The service was distributed as prepaid cards (similar to the prepaid cards used by the telecom service providers) thus gaining high distribution reach at minimum cost.

3.9 Challenges

The company needs to cross sell the service product (platform) developed to customers from varied industries to gain from economies of scale and scope. Thus, for example, in the F&A process, an accounts receivable process developed for a grocery retailer would need to be cross sold to customers within the industry and across other industries like mortgage service providers in order to have required economies of scale. However, the process developed may not be completely transferable creating challenges of customisation and sales.

Secondly, the small size of the clients being targeted (< US$100,000 turnover) makes it very difficult to develop a profitable customer acquisition model. Quatrro needs to keep the customer acquisition cost low which forces it to look for out-of-the-box solutions as it cannot maintain a dedicated sales force or fly its executives from India to the US on a regular basis. Thus, the company needed to develop an effective and scalable sales and distribution model so that it can acquire customers at low costs while targeting new customers who are not being currently served with innovative process platforms. Given the size of its target customers (SMBs), the company has been experimenting with its sales and distribution model which has been modified twice in the past three years. The company could not have a completely product-focused sales structure (based on service lines) as it would be very costly to maintain and the cost of customer acquisition would shoot up, while it could not hire only generalists as its solutions required domain and process knowledge for customer acquisition and management (cross selling). Therefore, the company has developed a hybrid sales structure.

Another related challenge that the company faces is how to cross sell its products to existing customers. For example, a risk management solution developed for a bank may not be perceived as totally relevant to a grocery retailer as a valuable product or as a business solution. Thus, identifying potential customers who are growth oriented and selling platform solutions developed for another domain (a bank, for instance) requires an innovative sales approach. Srinivas Pingali has grappled with these issues while preparing for his next new product offering which he is supposed to develop and launch into the US market in the next six months.

4
The Offshoring Industry in India: Moving Up the Value Chain?

Doris Rajakumari John

When American Express launched its Indian rupee card, the operations at its Indian division were revealing. The company found that the cost per transaction from India was significantly lower than those of the more advanced markets and that the quality of the output was also significantly superior. According to Raman Roy, touted as the father of the Indian outsourcing industry, who was in charge of the operations, 'The real gains were greater because of our execution efficiency, the number of first-call resolutions of customer problems, and the ease with which we resolved the issues (which was purely a function of our more qualified and better educated staff)' (Knowledge@ Wharton, 2003). Realising the substantial advantages of the Indian operations, John McDonald, the controller at American Express, soon added more responsibilities and the Indian unit became a key part of American Express' global operations. Overcoming a number of technological hurdles, Raman Roy, in charge of the Indian unit, was able to show superior work and also the resultant cost savings that were possible.

Soon a number of *Fortune 500* companies started offshoring their operations to India. Indian IT service providers also leveraged the offshoring boom and provided services to a number of clients, the majority of whom were based in the US. Over the years, the services offered shifted to more high-end ones, with foreign multinationals using India as their innovation base. However, some analysts were sceptical about the upward movement along the value chain and argued that the Indian offshoring industry had a long way to go. There was also a debate that India was losing its cost arbitrage to lower cost destinations. Other macroeconomic factors too affected this industry. In the wake of these challenges it remained to be seen how the future of the offshoring industry in India would evolve.

In the early 1980s, British Airways and other global airlines started conducting back-office operations in New Delhi. This was soon followed by firms like American Express that consolidated regional back-office operations in India. In 1985, Texas Instruments set up the first multinational technical design centre in Bangalore. Companies like General Electric (GE) took the lead and thus was born the offshoring story. By the late 1990s, the Y2K syndrome and the Internet boom drove up demand for IT services. During the same time, the increased investment in fibre optic infrastructure helped improve communications quality, and drive down the cost of communication. Ironically, the telecom and Internet bust in 2001–3 also drove growth in offshoring to India. Over the years, Western firms were looking to cut costs, and offshoring to India was a great cost-saving opportunity. One of the pioneers in India's offshoring boom was GE, which has been lauded for triggering the growth of the offshore outsourcing industry in India. 'GE has helped seed the growth of the entire Indian software services and BPO industry,' noted Mohan Sekhar, former chief delivery officer for iGate (De & Das, 2006).

4.1 General Electric (GE)

4.1.1 The GECIS experience

It was in September 1989 that Jack Welch the then Chairman of GE, flew to India hoping to sell products such as airplane engines, plastics and medical equipment to the Indian Government. During a breakfast meeting with top government advisers, including Sam Pitroda, the chief technology adviser to the late Indian Premier Rajiv Gandhi, and Jairam Ramesh, a senior economic adviser to India's ruling Congress party, it was Welch who got pitched. 'We want to sell you software,' Pitroda told a surprised Welch, explaining further that India needed business for its emerging high-tech sector. 'If I kiss your cheek, what do I get in return?' questioned the GE chairman, not sensing the outsourcing opportunity that he was about to discover (Solomon & Kranhold, 2005).

GE's tryst with India began way back in 1902, when it installed India's first hydropower plant. Later in 1930, International General

Electric (IGE) was set up for sales of GE products and services not represented in India. Its association continued in 1989, when GE Medical System partnered with Wipro Ltd, to manufacture and distribute a low-cost ultrasound machine. Although GE's industrial-equipment sales in India did not take off as anticipated, there was another development. Taking note of a cheap source of talented programmers and engineers, Chuck Pieper, GE Medical System's former Asia chief, set aside US$5 million annually to hire Wipro to write more software codes for GE ultrasound machines and CT scanners.

With the advent of the liberalisation era in 1991, GE looked at more Indian partners for its technology development, and Indian IT majors – including Wipro, Infosys and TCS – were some of the initial beneficiaries. With a clear mental map of its outsourcing requirements, GE considered its vendors as partners, investing long-term in them and believing in the vendors despite initial hiccups. GE had also given Indian companies access to all their training methodologies, both technical and managerial. The initial projects mainly involved mainframes and a few in the client–server space. This required intensive training and knowledge transfer, since at that time India was not a mainframe country. Other than big companies like Tata, nobody in India had mainframes and GE took the leap of faith with small companies, such as (at that time) the INR 5 crore Infosys, and invested heavily in developing the capabilities of its partners. GE brought in best practices and quality schemes to its vendors. The fact that India was host to more than 55 per cent of global SEI CMM Level 5 firms (a quality certification for software firms) could be attributed to this. However, with benefits of cost-cutting accruing, GE soon began playing one Indian software firm against another to drive down costs, demanding constant productivity gains. Recalling his experience, Ramesh Emani, who helped manage the software partnership said, 'GE was very brutal' (Solomon & Kranhold, 2005).

By the mid-1990s, top GE managers began encouraging other units to follow the medical division's lead in India. It was reported that in some cases, Welch himself gave instructions directly. 'For the same amount of engineering dollars, we were getting 50% more people thinking about stuff world-wide,' Pieper said (Solomon & Kranhold, 2005). By the late 1990s, GE began turning its attention from simply buying software from India to using the country as a base for data entry, processing credit card applications and other clerical tasks. Although companies such as American Express Co. and British Airways PLC had already moved some back-office operations to India, GE eventually went much further. Guided by Welch's ever-increasing appetite for cost-cutting, GE shifted thousands of jobs and operational expenses to India, an estimated annual savings of US$300 million.

In 1997 GE's financial unit was about to create an Indian office to provide support for its credit card venture in the US. Leveraging the availability of qualified labour at cheaper cost, GE realised that India's 100 million English speakers offered an inexpensive, educated labour pool for such tasks. Due to the absence of a third-party vendor for its non-core processes, GE was advised by consultants to establish a captive unit. This move would also help address some IP issues which would otherwise arise. Thus was born GE Capital International Services (GECIS) to provide internal support to GE units. Starting with a small team of 20 people, GECIS' first assignment was to process credit applications and comply with requests for change of address, telephone numbers and similar information for US clients. This data were processed and streamlined and later sent back to the US team.

Training its workforce in Six Sigma, the unit enhanced and refined its business processes outperforming GE's parent centres in the US, while reducing operating costs substantially, sometimes by half, at the same time. Roy, who was hired to spearhead GE's outsourcing operations said:

> We turned out much better quality on some assignments than was thought could be achieved. Errors per hundred and per thousand, turnaround times, accuracy, better understanding of what the customer wanted and delivering that, promise to pay versus actual payment – we judged the quality of our output on all these parameters, and of course the parameters differed from process to process. I found that, in general, we delivered superior quality and bettered existing benchmarks on many of these parameters.
>
> Knowledge@Wharton (2003)

By 1998, GECIS' employee headcount had grown to 800 and it was generating revenues up to US$4 million. The opportunity to take the unit to the next level – that is, from servicing batch transactions to handling online transactions – met with considerable resistance. A senior GE official once commented that 'call centres would never happen out of India' (Knowledge@Wharton, 2003). Many GE managers were sceptical about India's telephone and electricity infrastructure and did not believe that a captive in India could do the work. In the US, GE's executives were worried about replacing American workers with overseas labour and also feared that US clients might take offence at being called by foreigners.

Obsessed with nationalistic pride, Roy was determined to 'show what can happen out of India'. Roy's team worked with Indian regulators to install reliable phone lines and bought generators to guard against frequent power cuts. They strung bed sheets between cubicles to meet US requirements for privacy of financial data. Recalling his dialogue with the phone company, Roy said, 'The phone company initially told me there wouldn't be outages for much longer than six minutes ... I told them I couldn't survive an outage of even six seconds' (Solomon & Kranhold, 2005). The venture offered clear economic advantages. An Indian call-centre worker earned on average around US$3000 annually, compared with more than US$27,000 earned by their US counterpart.

As the cost savings, efficiencies and quality became apparent, GE increasingly came to view outsourcing as a tool to drive up its profits, and moved more processes to India. At GE's annual gathering of top management, Welch challenged his top managers to meet with the Indian staff to learn about the advantages of outsourcing. Pitching their operations, GECIS managers challenged other GE units that they weren't full-fledged players if they weren't doing something in India (Solomon & Kranhold, 2005).

After the call centre trial in early 1999, GE allocated more than US$10 million to expand the operation, as well as other processes. In the following year, GECIS India started adding high-value products to its portfolio and undertook more complex, higher-priced and strategically important work. Revenues had increased to US$85 million and by 2001, GECIS' headcount had doubled to 10,000 from the previous year, and more than 500 processes had been moved from Europe, America and Australia. The company had about 700 chartered accountants on its roll, and GECIS India was processing transactions in 28 different currencies (Patel, 2007). GECIS businesses in India were structured as nine centres of excellence (CoEs), broadly divided into financial BPOs, non-financial BPOs and high-value processes.

Until the September 11, 2001 terrorist attacks in the US, GECIS had worked on a 70:70:70 metric, meaning that 70 per cent of all tasks were outsourced, 70 per cent of outsourced tasks were offshored and 70 per cent of offshored work went to India. However, after the crisis, GE planned to expand its presence in other countries. To diversify risks, it opened new centres in China and Hungary. By early 2003, GECIS had become a mature unit, handling high-end, complex business for the company and attaining high-revenue growth. GECIS contributed to cost savings of 40–50 per cent annually (around US$300 million yearly) for GE. According to Welch, GECIS was a key driver of the company's growth between 1998 and 2001, saving GE US$1 billion in operational costs. By 2004, GECIS had 17,500 employees and revenues of US$426 million, and around 700 processes had migrated to India. The offshore services ranged from call centres, insurance claims processing and accounts payable to highly complex processes such as supply chain management, logistics, analytics and actuarial tasks. After attaining high growth and utilisation rates, however, GECIS' cost advantage began a gradual decline. By 2002–3, GE realised that several third-party outsourcing companies in India could do the work more cheaply than GECIS. During this time, GE also restructured its core businesses and found that GECIS no longer matched its core competency. So in 2003, GE began to consider spinning off its BPO business and started pitching for third-party business. In December 2004, GE sold a 60 per cent stake to private equity firms General Atlantic Partners and Oak Hill Capital for about US$500 million, and GECIS became an independent entity with global headquarters in India. GE retained a 40 per cent stake for business continuity reasons and committed to outsource from GECIS under a multiyear contract (Patel, 2007).

After the spin-off in October 2005, GECIS changed its name to Genpact. It also expanded its operations in India, opening a fifth office in Kolkata and by the end of the fiscal year in December 2005, Genpact recorded revenues of US$493 million, with GE accounting for 85 per cent of this amount. 'We are mission-critical to GE,' said Pramod Bhasin, Genpact's president. According to him, GE's 700 business processes done in India saved the company US$340 million a year. Driven by the best practices of GE, Genpact focussed on scale and geography, critical to the offshore outsourcing business. With its sales network spread across the globe, Genpact was poised for steady growth. Being the only US$1 billion-plus India-based BPO company, Genpact posted revenues of US$1.04 billion for the year ending 2008, recording a growth of 26 per cent over the previous year. With around 80 per cent of its business coming from existing customers, Genpact's COO V. N. Tyagarajan commented that the company had been able to mine its existing customers much better to get higher revenues and in the process moved up the value chain. For the year 2009, Genpact said it was confident of achieving a 10–15 per cent growth in revenue. GE continued to be one of Genpact's largest customers accounting for 47 per cent of its revenue for 2008. From assessing insurance claims to devising statistical models to helping GE sales staff understand the needs, strengths and weaknesses of customers and rivals; preparing data for GE annual reports; writing enterprise resource-planning software; and processing US$35 billion worth of global invoices, Genpact's services were critical to GE (Thimmaya, 2009).

GE also became the first foreign conglomerate to offshore its in-house legal work to India. Its GE Plastics unit hired a lawyer to write and review contracts with vendors. According to the company, the move saved the company US$500,000 in 2001 and US$700,000 in 2002. Its GE Consumer Finance unit also used an Indian legal team. GE had also established the GE-India Design Centre (Satyam GE Software Services) as a joint venture between GE Industrial Systems and Satyam Computer Services Ltd in 1999. The venture designed and developed new products related to industrial systems using CAD/CAE and software solutions in the areas of embedded systems, e-commerce and human machine interface.

4.1.2 The John F. Welch Technology Centre (JFWTC)

The year 2000 marked another giant step for GE's Indian operations when it opened the John F. Welch Technology Centre (JFWTC) in Bangalore. Spread over 50 acres of land, the US$175 million, one million square feet centre housed modern laboratories and facilities to conduct research and development (R&D) for GE businesses worldwide. The facility had grown from just 275 employees to about 4300 employees in nine years. A multidisciplinary R&D centre, it collaborated with GE's three other R&D facilities: GE Global Research, GE Technology Infrastructure (aircraft engines, locomotives and signalling, health care and enterprise solutions) and GE Energy Infrastructure (steam/gas turbines, wind energy, oil and gas, water and process technologies) that formed the GE Global Research team. Apart from India, the team operated from New York, Germany and China to conduct research, development and engineering activities for all of GE's diverse businesses worldwide.

Almost exactly resembling GE's global research facility in New York, JFWTC boasted a large number of scientists with Ph.D.s engaged in fundamental research. 'More than 60% of our people have Masters and PhD degrees. And 20% are part of the reverse brain [drain] – they've given up jobs in the USA to return to India,' noted the centre's managing director, Guillermo Wille, one of the centre's few non-Indians (Ganguly, 2007). The centre worked on a variety of assignments: redesigning turbine-engine blades, scrutinising the molecular structure of materials to be used in DVDs for short-term use in which the movie is automatically erased after a few days and devising ways to boost output in a GE plastics plant in Spain by 20 per cent. As of 2009, the engineers at JFWTC had filed more than 850 patents in the US since the centre's inception in 2000.

'The game here really isn't about saving costs but to speed innovation and generate growth for the company,' explained Wille. The centre's operation had become increasingly vital to the future of the company. For instance, engineers at JFWTC reduced the noise generated by a wind farm of around 100 windmills from an ear-splitting 85 decibels to a more manageable 80 decibels. Though small, the 5 decibel reduction represented a 'quantum change' in wind energy technology. T. P. Chopra, CEO and president of GE India declared that 'The Centre has shaped up beyond our expectations. All our businesses are asking us to do more high-end work and they are quite happy to allocate the funds' (Sachitanand, 2008a). Though the centre focussed initially on plastics research, it has grown to reflect GE's quest to be seen as an innovator. 'Starting with Thomas Alva Edison, innovation is a big deal for us,' Wille said. In tune with its strategy to launch 'ecomagination' products, from which the company expected to get around US$25 billion in revenues by 2010, GE had invested US$700 million in product development in 2005 and upped this to US$1.5 billion in 2007. Wille explained that under the 'ecomagination' strategy, the centre hoped to launch products that caused 'less pollution, more efficiency and more power in smaller packages', while undertaking 'core research in all product-based businesses'.

The Engineering Design and Development Centre of GE Transportation-India at JFWTC was working on developments specifically in the railroads and signalling business. The unit was involved in the development of a lighter 5000 horsepower locomotive that would bear only 22½ tonnes per axle compared to 32½ tonnes borne by those run in the US. They were also involved in developing a hybrid locomotive that would reuse the energy generated by a machine going downstream to recharge batteries and increase efficiency. 'Building the locomotive is simple; getting the battery to absorb and discharge this energy quickly continues to be a challenge,' said Upender Nanda, the general manager of the unit. His division had also become a global hub for train signalling or in 'developing algorithms that allow coaches and trains to be as close together as possible without touching each other' (Sachitanand, 2008a).

JFWTC had played a key role in designing and building high-strength fan blades for the GE90 engine that powered the Boeing 787 Dreamliner. The engineers were faced with the dual challenge of 'making sure that the engine could run at full thrust for long periods and as part of its green focus, decrease the fuel it consumes'. 'We have flown one million hours of safe flight and weathered 16 bird hits too ... we helped decrease fuel consumption by at least 20 per cent,' said Damodhar Padhi, the general manager of India Engineering Operations at the Bangalore Engineering Centre (Sachitanand, 2008a).

At another unit engineers worked on key innovations in gasification, to improve the production of clean power from coal, a key energy source for much of the developing world. Engineers at the unit had been able to reduce product development time by 66 per cent and were declared a centre of excellence in gasification. JFWTC also focussed on producing products and solutions for emerging economies. For instance, the Water and Process Technology Team developed molecules to separate fat and water when meat was processed. Through this process, the meat and fat recovered could be sold and the water recovered could be reused. The team had also developed chemicals that could separate water from oil and this helped eliminate water which was a pollutant in crude oil refining. The team's lead, C. Maltesh, noted the unit's success, 'We have been able to get two patents for our technology and bagged customers in the US and India' (Sachitanand, 2008a).

JFWTC was also involved in health care and medical research, with scientists working on reinventing current diagnostic tools, such as X-ray and ECG to suit developing markets. One of these reinventions was a portable ECG machine, the MAC 400, which was smaller than an average laptop and worked on battery power, and did not need handling by a doctor to diagnose the images. The unique device helped bring down the cost of an ECG down from INR 1000 to INR 50. Health care was one of the thrust areas for GE, and it had earmarked US$6 billion globally to come up with affordable health care solutions for developing countries. A battery powered X-ray machine that could take 100 images per charge and hence could be deployed in remote rural areas was also developed (Sachitanand, 2008a). Another diagnostic technology allowed doctors to eliminate multiple layers of body tissue to quickly locate and identify a potentially serious illness. This was both more efficient and less invasive for the patient.

Some of the other innovations developed at JFWTC included a transparent heat-resistant polycarbonate plastic that aimed to replace the glass used in car head lamps, evolved plastics that go into new generation laptops and cell phones, a washing machine that used half the normal amount of water, and a generator with reduced vibrations (Ganguly, 2007). JFWTC's major innovations are listed in Table 4.1.

JFWTC is one of GE's largest R&D operations, with an annual research expenditure of US$4 billion, around 2.5 per cent of GE's annual revenues. As of 2009, GE has invested US$175 million in the centre. 'Our scientists have helped shrink the new product development cycle in every business area that GE is in,' noted Wille. The centre has helped cut the go-to-market time drastically, sometimes even up to 50 per cent. With other foreign MNCs like Shell, GM and Pratt & Whitney (GE's arch-rival in aircraft engines) setting up similar research centres in India, Wille was aware that unless the centre continued to achieve more breakthroughs, it would be increasingly difficult to attract the best talent. The centre was also faced with the challenge of coordinating with GE's research units around the globe. 'This is where the challenge lies – the time zone differences, cultural differences and language,' observed Chopra, GE's India head

Table 4.1 Innovations at JFWTC

Pedestrian safety bumper	It had collapsible energy absorbers made of Xenoy resin and was positioned behind a vehicle's frontage. It collapsed on impact.
Advanced combustor system	Reduced NOx emission and increased efficiency of fuel burn by 20% for GE's GEnx aircraft engine.
HF X-ray	Developed for the Indian market, it used a high-frequency X-ray generator to offer high quality X-ray images at low cost.
GE Evolution series locomotives	It was one of the cleanest diesel-electric locomotives ever built. It generated 16 cylinders' worth of power with only 12, and cuts emissions by 40%.
Smart axle counter system	Developed for Indian Railways, it helped tell whether a trolley or a train has been stationed at the platform.
MAC 400 ECG	It could take 100 ECGs with a completely charged battery.
Component design	For the H turbine, which was the world's most efficient gas turbine.
AutoBone Xpress	An image analysis software that helped doctors get a better 3-D image of bony structures.
Dual-flame stacked burner	The design incorporated two layers of flames by having two rings one above the other, offering more heating capacity without increasing the size of the burners.
Wind farm design and analysis	This was called micrositing and was a special software tool developed to help customers optimise the output from windmills.
A battery-operated printer	Developed for the Karnataka State Road Transport Corporation.
The roof of the Shanghai South railway station	Used Multiwall sheets.

Source: Compiled from Sangani (2009).

(Sachitanand, 2008a). The centre was expected to expand rapidly, with every fourth GE technologist operating out of India by 2010.

4.1.3 India as GE's manufacturing base

'Following the GECIS and the technology centre experience, India will now be a manufacturing base, too,' stated Chopra (Ramana,

2009). In October 2009 at GE Day, an annual two-day event in Hyderabad, the company announced that it would be setting up a wind turbine manufacturing plant in South India by mid-2010. Hitherto the company had a presence in manufacturing primarily through local partners. Chopra explained that while 'initially the company would be working with supply chain partners globally and assembling the units in India, it would, over time, develop a local supply chain and indigenise production' (Sangani, 2009). GE plans to grow primarily in health care, energy and infrastructure through a clear three-pronged strategic approach. The approach would be a mix of localisation of products and services, and public–private partnerships (PPP) with the state on defence and infrastructure projects.

GE already has connections with many state and private companies in India. GE Capital has linked up with the State Bank of India, India's largest public sector bank for its credit card operations and with Bharat Heavy Electricals Ltd (BHEL), a public sector equipment manufacturer, for its gas turbines. In 2009, it had also signed an agreement with BHEL to float a joint venture to manufacture diesel locomotives for the Indian Railways. It has also collaborated with L&T for power generation and with Wipro for health care. GE was enlisted as a validated end user (VEU) by the US government, which gave it permission to sell advanced defence technology to specific Indian institutions. With the signing of the India–US nuclear deal, GE expected to do substantial work on nuclear energy by 2010. Given GE's commitment to going green, developing nuclear energy was going to be key focus area for the company. GE had little exposure in the renewable energy space and hoped to strengthen it through working on nuclear energy in India (Sangani, 2009).

Although GE had deferred its target of achieving revenues of US$8 billion in India by 2010 because of the global economic slowdown, its chairman and CEO, Jeffrey Immelt emphasised that India continued to play a key role in GE's growth plans and was looking at new business models in India. 'We need to be looking to design and engineer products in India that meet the needs of the Indian market, and then look for opportunities to sell these products in other markets,' he said. Referring to the low cost ECG device that's developed for the emerging economies but is being sold in the US, he added that 'if GE's businesses are to survive and prosper in the next decade, they must become as adept at reverse innovation as they are at glocalisation' (Mahanta, 2009). For the fiscal year 2008–9 GE India's revenue was US$2.6 billion.

4.2 IBM

4.2.1 Delivery networks

Another foreign multinational that was making rapid strides in India was IBM. It re-entered India in 1992 through a Tata joint venture named Tata Information Systems Ltd. In 1999 IBM India was established as a wholly owned subsidiary of IBM Corporation. Although initially, IBM's Indian operations were focussed on product sales, it later shifted towards services. This strategic shift to software and services led to a rapid rise in its Indian presence. Its work force in India had increased from 9000 in 2003 to over 100,000 in 2009. In the company's first-ever analyst meet outside the US, in Bangalore in 2006, IBM chief executive Sam Palmisano announced an investment of US$6 billion in India, over the following three years. Spanning everything from research to innovative delivery models and education, it was the largest single investment by any multinational tech company in India. The company had already invested US$2 billion in the previous three years. Palmisano noted that 'if you are not here in India, making the right investments, finding and developing the best employees and business partners, you won't be able to combine the country, the skills and expertise with that from around the world. The investment will ensure that we make the most of the opportunities to grow in this market' (Rai, 2006). IBM had also become a multinational with the largest number of employees in India.

Unable to counter competition from low-cost Indian tech companies, this move to focus on India was critical for IBM. The company, however, said that cost arbitrage alone was not the reason for its ramp-up. Commenting on the phenomenal growth in its employee numbers in India, Larry Longseth, vice-president of server systems operations at the company's strategic outsourcing unit said, 'We're putting the highest level of skills in India' (Hamm, 2006). IBM's strategy was to increasingly make India form part of the company's globally integrated operations, an initiative to augment its competitive edge. Through this globalisation strategy that aimed at revamping its people supply chain, IBM reorganised its 200,000-strong services workforce along skill lines, and not just geography (*Bloomberg Businessweek*, 5 June 2006). It would then coordinate operations worldwide to deliver services that were better as well as cheaper. For instance, in the past, many software installations for clients' PCs were done for each machine individually by an IT employee who personally inspected each machine. The average cost incurred in such a case was about US$70 per PC. With the shift to the globalisation strategy, IBM would execute the same activity through a team of 200 employees in Toronto running a software installation factory for clients worldwide. They assembled packages that were delivered to machines over the net and the cost of this operation was just 20 cents per PC. 'Some people think the world is centred in India, and that's it. Globalisation is more than that. Our customers need us to put the right skills in the right place at the right time,' commented Robert W. Moffat Jr, the senior vice-president and the person in charge of the makeover (*Bloomberg Businessweek*, 5 June 2006).

IBM would also use India to increase its scientific research capabilities, which gave it an edge over its Indian competitors. India, along with its global services and research organisations, would play a role in bringing automation to impact its services. Out of the 15 projects that were underway, two of them were being piloted in Bangalore at the IBM research lab. 'Bangalore is our living lab where we take new technologies and processes and deploy them. Once we test them there we'll deploy them around the globe,' said Mahmoud Naghshineh, the director of service delivery for IBM Research (Hamm, 2006). IBM India's global delivery centres, equipped with the latest data centre management systems, and using the most advanced business processes, would help the company in its 'on demand business' strategy. Through this initiative the company expected to transform the way it operated, reduce costs, improve customer service, reduce risk, and improve speed and agility in the marketplace. IBM was one of the leading global companies that offered end-to-end solutions to the customers from hardware to software, services and consulting.

As a result of its globalisation strategy and integration of India into its worldwide operations, IBM was able to eliminate 20,000 jobs in high-cost markets such as the US, Europe and Japan. The success of this strategy was also reflected in its second-quarter 2007 revenues, which were up 9 per cent, to US$23.8 billion, including a 10 per cent increase in revenue at its IT services group, which was under intense competition from its Indian rivals. Soon IBM became a leader in the Indian tech services industry, with a 10 per cent share of the domestic market. It had made deals with a number of blue-chip clients, including Bharti Airtel Ltd, the leading cellular carrier; the real estate developer DLF; the state-run Canara Bank; and the Indian tax department. One of the reasons for IBM's success in India was explained by the then NASSCOM President Kiran Karnik, 'IBM has really understood what India is all about' (Kripalani, 2007). It has been winning deals in India faster than any of its local competitors. In the first half of 2007 alone, it signed deals worth US$1.4 billion in long-term contracts. The ten-year agreement signed with Bharti Airtel in 2004 was worth US$750 million and increased to over US$2 billion in 2009. Through the deal, IBM provided Bharti Airtel the technical support it needed to take full advantage of its future flexibility and growth potential by adopting a business-driven framework for integration. This allowed Airtel to implement and deliver new services rapidly, and helped it process 1.5 million new customers per month.

Apart from signing deals with blue chips, IBM also focussed on the small and medium enterprises (SMEs) market. IBM was one of the first companies to recognise the opportunity among SMEs in the early 1990s. Since then it has invested in the development of products and services specifically priced and designed for the SME marketplace under the brand name 'IBM Express Portfolio.' IBM also introduced the SME Toolkit, a free programme that enabled entrepreneurs and small businesses to learn how to implement sustainable business management practices needed for growth in various domain areas. With more than 50 per cent of its revenue coming from its SME operations, IBM had moved into Tier II cities throughout India to focus on the SME market. Spurred by IBM's success, Indian rivals started to look for more opportunities from Indian companies after years of focusing on customers overseas (Shivkamal, 2008). Commenting on competition, Shanker Annaswamy, IBM's India chief said that 'Competition is welcome ... No one has the depth we do' (*Bloomberg Businessweek*, 3 September 2007). Although IBM could not match its Indian rivals on price, analysts believed that the company's vast resources of technology and expertise, including its Indian workforce, would help bridge the gap. These other factors gave IBM a competitive edge. Over the years, IBM India has expanded its footprint and set up the complete range of its services capabilities, including consulting and systems integration, infrastructure, applications, and business process transformation and management in India.

4.2.2 IBM Research India

The first IBM Research Lab in India was established in April 1998 within the IIT campus in Delhi, making it the youngest of IBM's eight globally integrated research labs. These labs had become a source of innovation on a range of IBM's business portfolios, from software to semiconductors to supercomputers. An additional lab was opened in Bangalore in 2005, with both labs focussing on a wide array of research areas blending pure and applied research. Worldwide, IBM has registered the highest number of patents (averaging 9.3 patents per day) and its IBM Research Laboratory (IBMRL) is known for devising carbon nanotubes and computer languages such as Fortran (Sachitanand, 2008b). Its researchers had even been awarded the Nobel Prize for Physics for their work in the area of high-temperature superconductivity. IBM had earned 4186 US patents in 2008, becoming the first company ever to earn more than 4000 US patents in a single year. For the 16th consecutive year IBM had led the global patent leadership over companies such as Microsoft, Hewlett-Packard, Oracle, Apple, EMC, Accenture and Google.

The Indian Research unit focussed on conceptual research in areas such as telecommunications and global delivery of IT services from the two centres. 'Our research is helping the services business create new offerings, optimise service delivery through better automation and knowledge management, as well as improve governance through analytics', said Guruduth Banavar, director of IBM Research Labs (Sachitanand, 2008b). According to Banavar, the Indian labs work on specific requirements from the services division and the products they develop are often utilised in IBM's next-generation solutions. IBMRL has many centres of excellence with expertise in areas including information and knowledge management, interaction and collaboration technologies, systems management, distributed and high-performance computing, programming technologies and software engineering, analytics and optimisations, services innovation, and telecommunications. Some of the research projects conducted at the Indian research labs in 2009 include semantics-based system monitoring solutions, integration of structured and unstructured information, speech recognition in Hindi, autonomic computing, model-driven business transformation and business intelligence for CRM solutions, and semantics extraction from low entropy text (IBMa, 2009).

One of the most critical breakthroughs for IBM was its work on the Spoken Web. IBM's Mobile Web initiative was based out of India and relied upon the help of experts in eight labs in six countries. 'The Spoken Web project aims to transform how people interact with e-commerce sites by using speech, rather than the written word. The Spoken Web is the World Wide Web in a telecom network, where people can create and browse "VoiceSites" and traverse "Voice Links",' said Guruduth Banavar (Sachitanand, 2008b). Another research team, for instance, developed a web-based program that analysed a person's accent, grammar and vocabulary. This package was used to screen job applicants at IBM's call centre operations but had further applications, including testing language fluency. The centre had also contributed to the Blue Gene supercomputer project spearheaded by IBM's global research units (IBMb, 2009). In addition to this futuristic research, the IBM Software Labs were involved in devising on-ground applications and solutions for customers. 'Besides buying our products and solutions, our customers want to use their technology infrastructure to improve business processes. We've devised innovative solutions for customers of all sizes and across many industries,' said Annaswamy, MD of IBM India (Sachitanand, 2008b).

4.2.3 IBM Daksh

To further strengthen its delivery capabilities in India, IBM acquired Daksh eServices (Daksh) for US$150 million in 2004. Acclaimed as one of the best-managed Indian BPO service providers, Daksh's acquisition was expected to enhance IBM's business transformation capabilities in areas including customer relationship management (CRM) and financial management services in key industries such as banking, insurance, retail, technology, telecommunications, travel and transportation. Besides, the initiative was also expected to increase the scope of IBM's global network of 22 business transformation delivery centres, adding capabilities in India and the Philippines. During the time of acquisition, 80 per cent of Daksh's revenue came from voice and web support. According to Gartner, the research agency, Daksh focussed on e-commerce, retail, consumer electronics and telecom verticals and boasted clients such as Amazon, Yahoo and Sprint.

Since its acquisition, IBM Daksh had been able to offer services integrating IBM's capabilities across research, development and consulting into high-value solutions to its clients. For example, IBM Daksh had successfully leveraged IBM's research capabilities to develop a text-analytics tool called ProACT, which automated the analysis of customer satisfaction surveys to improve the real-time effectiveness of email-based customer help desk operations. Another technology that was developed was a software application that combed through the information collected from customers by call centre operators, identified potential problems and alerted clients in a matter of days so that they could deal with them quickly.

Leveraging IBM's research and consulting skills, IBM Daksh attracted growing outsourcing businesses from *Fortune 500* clients. Some assignments included innovating and managing business operations for a leading US health insurance company, a UK internet service provider, a global consumer goods leader, one of the world's top telecommunications companies and a major airline (*The Hindu Business Line*, 3 June 2006). In 2008, it struck a high profile deal with MakeMyTrip, which was followed by a deal with Airtel. Some earlier deals signed by IBM where handed over to IBM Daksh, a notable one being a deal with the Union Bank of India that was signed in 2007. IBM Daksh was shifting towards high-value services, new geographies and even new verticals. It moved into analytics, supported by IBM's strong expertise and it also started risk analytics practice and legal services outsourcing. Its strategy to leverage parentage and pitch for integrated deals resulted in increasing revenue growth.

With IBM India's revenues having crossed US$1 billion by 2008 and having emerged as a top player in the Indian IT market, India had become well established as a conduit for innovation and path-breaking research in IBM's global business model (Sachitanand, 2008b). In response to recessionary climate in 2008–9, IBM was expected to cut about 5000 jobs in the US and shift them to India, despite the option of hiring in the US at much lower salaries than before. IBM wanted to exploit the lower cost factors in India and this was an important part of its offshoring strategy (McIntyre, 2009). IBM's share of the local outsourcing market was also expected to increase from a 36 per cent market share in 2009 to 50 per cent in 2010 (Mishra, 2009).

4.3 Indian IT service providers

The role of Indian IT service providers in the offshore outsourcing boom has been no less phenomenal. Predicted to reach US$60–2 billion by FY2011 from US$31.4 billion in FY2007, Indian IT exporters were cautious in their predictions in light of the economic recession. Industry body, NASSCOM, was however positive about growth and they reported that 'Despite the unprecedented economic downturn, the industry will witness sustainable growth. The global technology spending outlook for 2009 is affected by the recessionary environment but it is expected to grow from 2010' (*The Economic Times*, 4 March 2009). According to the trade body, exports for fiscal year 2009–10 were estimated to reach US$47 billion.

Evolving from handling Y2K-related projects in the late 1990s, Indian IT service providers moved onto focussing on Internet application development during the dot-com bust and later matured into handling newer services like remote infrastructure management, enterprise package implementation, IT consulting and business process outsourcing. The verticals serviced has also gone beyond banking and financial services, which was one of the first movers, and built up expertise in areas like health care, media and entertainment, telecom, travel and aviation. The revenues in these sectors has also increased across various verticals. A number of factors has influenced this growth, building on India's unique value proposition. These factors include breadth of service offering, quality/maturity of processes, cost advantage, ease of scalability, global and 24/7 delivery capability, IT infrastructure and local talent.

Driven by the mantra that cost arbitrage alone is not sufficient to sustain growth, Indian IT companies have constantly tried to provide value-added services to their clients. For instance, even during the early days of development in the sector, companies like Spectramind provided a service called 'Knowledge Acquisition' which was separate from basic services like email management, inbound and outbound voice processes, and customer relationship management. Under this service, the company provided high-end consulting services in areas like biotechnology and hired scientists holding doctoral degrees in molecular biology and genomics. They also built a knowledge base that would help scientists across the globe reduce the time spent in hypothesising, data collection and then validating findings. A quality control processes for their clients' knowledge management system was also established (Srikanth, 2002).

Focussing on different niche verticals such as accounting and geographic information system (GIS), HCL's eServe trained local accountants in US GAAP accounting practices so that they could handle the entire accounting process of global companies. Another service provider, MsourcE, which handled inbound customer service calls for debit cards, moved into handling claims investigation, a domain-specific function. MsourcE had also developed software to provide information on ATM locations to customers, based on where they were located (Srikanth, 2002). The strategy behind many of these transactions was to enter a deal as a low-cost service provider and then scale up the value chain.

Operating through its subsidiary, Progeon (later renamed Infosys BPO Limited), Infosys made a foray into the BPO sector, focussing on the less-explored and comparatively riskier non-voice market which included data centres and record management. At a time when BPO meant voice-based businesses, this was a significant move. Over the years, non-voice contributed up to 20 per cent of Infosys' revenues. Its business model is one of delivering low-cost IT and BPO services from mainly low-cost locations, combined with its high-margin consulting business. Infosys BPO has also moved up the value chain by adding analytics, re-engineering processes and upgrading its skills. Among the 300 processes that it offers, it has developed one that could monitor network faults and take corrective action from its Indian centre (Rattanani, 2007). Its research arm, the Software Engineering and Technology Labs (SETLabs), was the centre for applied technology research in software engineering and enterprise technology and by 2009 Infosys had filed 196 patent applications. Infosys also made a mark in handling specialised engineering design work for clients such as Airbus and Boeing. British Telecom (BT), one of Infosys' largest clients, contributed 9.1 per cent of total revenues in FY2008.

The offering of value-added services was also true of other Indian IT giants like Tata Consultancy Services (TCS) and Wipro. For instance, Wipro's deal with the Australian company, Origin Energy, resulted in Wipro performing high-end technology and process transformation work. Through a centre established in Melbourne, Wipro serviced nearly ten large local contracts utilising 300 employees in Australia and 200 in India. The trend of shifting to offer KPO services was already evident in the Indian market. With buyers realising higher margins at the higher-end of the value chain, and scarcity of highly trained specialised talent pool in the developed countries, KPO services grew fast in India. New verticals such as animation, publishing and law were also emerging.

Despite signs that Indian service providers were moving up the value chain, some analysts were sceptical. They argued that Indian players had not fully leveraged areas such as business consulting, a domain dominated for decades by firms such as IBM and Accenture, and needed to invest heavily to secure a position in this arena. Although firms such as Accenture were much bigger compared to Indian IT firms such as Wipro, the pricing of Wipro was roughly half that of Accenture's. According to Manoj Mohta, head of Crisil Research, 'The inability of Indian tier-I players to offer premium service lines such as consulting, system integration is exacerbated by the limited effort towards developing intellectual property-based products' (*Businessworld*, 26 January 2008).

India has made significant progress in launching branded products but still has a long way to go to be comparable to their foreign counterparts. As of 2009, over 600 MNCs had carried out product R&D through their subsidiaries in India. A major challenge in the enhancement of this trend was the quality of talent available. The available talent pool in the Indian software product business was rated low on product architecture and management, product marketing, user interface and design, as well as release and configuration, all of which are critical for the software product business (Krishnakumar, 2008a).

4.4 Road ahead

Although cost arbitrage with respect to talent sourcing has been one of the most important factors in fuelling the offshoring boom, the gap is slowly closing with increasing salary levels in India. On an average, salaries in the Indian ITS/ITES industry have increased by 15–20 per cent between 2003 and 2008 The underlying reason for the increasing salary costs was the disparity in the demand and supply of high-quality talent. It was projected that India would need a 2.3 million-strong IT and BPO workforce by 2010 to maintain its market share in the global market. Despite India having the third largest higher education capacity in the world and producing almost three million graduates every year, only 25 per cent of Indian engineering graduates had the skills to be directly employed in IT jobs, and only 10 per cent of fresh Indian graduates were suitable for BPO jobs, and further, only 50 per cent of the suitable pool were willing to join the IT/BPO industry. It was predicted that lack of focus to counter these issues would lead to a shortage of 0.8–1.2 million entry-level graduates by 2012. To address this, the industry was taking corrective action. Efforts were being taken to expand the number of people willing to join the industry, improving the quality of the workforce through focused initiatives, and matching jobs more closely with employee profiles to reduce attrition rates (Souza, 2008).

Middle-management personnel would also be in short supply and sector-specific skill shortages, such as actuaries for insurance BPOs, were also likely to emerge. Also, with approximately 50 per cent of the additional talent requirements of the fresh, entry-level pool likely to be available in Tier II and III cities in India, access would become difficult, due to the geographic distribution of employable talent. This in turn would necessitate creation of physical and social infrastructure in these cities.

Even with these challenges, India continues to be viewed as the most cost-competitive destination when compared to other offshore destinations. It maintains its edge through a unique combination of high people skills, favourable business environment and low cost (Kundu, 2004). According to an A. T. Kearney study, India not only has remained at the forefront of the outsourcing industry but has also become an enabler for industry growth through expansion of Indian offshoring firms into other countries (A. T. Kearney Study, 2009). Shrewd management and innovation has enabled Indian service providers to offset salary increases by reductions in facility-related expenses, and significant improvements in operational efficiencies including automation, reuse of program components, better utilisation of bench strength, onsite–offshore integration, process maturity and project management skills. However, Indian companies have to contend with newer service delivery geographies that are emerging with niche capabilities. Apart from the Philippines, Vietnam and Latin America, destinations in the Middle East and North Africa are emerging as key offshoring regions. Many of these other destinations such as the Latin American countries, have an advantage over India of being located closer to vendors in Europe and the US, and also provide Spanish language capability as an added advantage. With near-shoring becoming increasingly popular for processes requiring the same time-zone presence, some of these destinations could prove more attractive than India.

Responding to this trend, Indian IT companies have already begun looking at new markets to reorganise their product portfolios and offer new service lines. Tier I firms such as Infosys and Wipro are expected to expand their global footprints and open delivery centres in China, Latin America, Eastern Europe and North America. To cut costs, it is expected that large clients would move towards single vendor sourcing as opposed to sourcing for specific requirements, which tend to cost more. As clients increasingly prefer to outsource multiple processes to a single vendor, firms that provide an entire range of services stand to benefit the most (Krishnakumar, 2008b).

Another shift in trend is said to be towards the domestic Indian market. The domestic IT-BPO market was expected to reach INR 1113 billion (US$24.3 billion) in FY2009. Domestic services showed signs of increasing sophistication as building enterprise IT infrastructures and applications, networking and communication became key priorities for India Inc. In FY2009, domestic IT services spends were estimated to grow 20 per cent to touch INR 380 billion (US$8.3 billion). The software product segment registered a growth of 15 per cent (INR 103 billion/US$2.3 billion), and the domestic BPO segment recorded the fastest growth of about 40 per cent to reach INR 88.7 billion (US$1.9 billion) (NASSCOM, 2009). In response to this, Indian IT companies like Infosys said they would start bidding for domestic businesses, admitting that the 'home market has reached a level of maturity'. Suresh Vaswani, joint CEO of Wipro's IT business, agreed with this assessment: 'There is scope to drive transformation across all verticals. We are fairly ambitious about the opportunity with telecom service providers, retailers, government, healthcare, infrastructure and banking. There are deals to be won in aerospace and manufacturing also. So the opportunity is broad-based, and we need to seize it' (*Businessworld*, 26 January 2008). According to Gartner, Indian companies in the private and state sector, from banks to railways, were expected to spend an estimated US$5 billion on new technology between 2008 and 2010.

There is also a growing trend of establishing BPO operations in rural areas. Wipro and Infosys were planning to start domestic BPO operations in smaller towns and rural areas to offer native language-based capabilities and data entry services. Compared to average billing rates of US$8–12 per hour to international clients, it is around US$3–4 per hour for every employee in the BPO sector for domestic clients. The rural shift would generate job opportunities at low costs but the enterprise is limited by availability of skilled manpower, broadband connectivity and frequent power cuts. Tier I companies like Infosys and Wipro were looking to tie up with rural BPO operators such as RuralShores, DesiCrew, Sai BPO and HOV Services.

The other sectors to gain significance are the SMEs who are expected to look increasingly towards outsourcing to stave off cost pressures to survive. This segment was previously ignored by the larger vendors. 'During the times of 40–50% growth rates, the large Indian vendors had become picky in terms of client and deal sizes, but any such filters have blown out of the window. In the present circumstances, vendors will be only too happy to serve SMEs', said Nishant Verma, vice-president of Tholons Capital (*Businessworld*, 26 January 2008). While large mergers and acquisition deals are expected to slow down, Tier I companies like Infosys, Wipro, TCS and HCL, are expected to acquire smaller firms to plug gaps in their portfolios and gain client proximity. Due to the recessionary environment, smaller players are finding the going tough, and are more open to mergers or takeovers to survive. Although the economic crisis has brought in a shift in trend on various aspects, the fundamental motivation for offshoring has not diminished – in fact it has become stronger.

For brand India, however, to capitalise on the emerging opportunities, the Indian industry has to work with clients to enhance the cost value proposition. This would involve additional investments in building capability across employees, domain knowledge, functional and technical skills, and an increase in their global delivery footprint. While Indian IT-BPO firms are adept in driving efficiencies through automation and process improvements, the companies have to understand that they would need to deliver a more significant impact on client businesses, through solutions that are innovative and transformative in nature. These enhanced, innovative solutions would also enable companies to access new market segments, deliver new service lines and create in-house IP in emerging technology areas. Although their revenue dependency on the US has considerably reduced, they have to look to new opportunities in Europe and the Asia-Pacific region.

The Indian government also has a significant role to play. Infrastructural development work needs to be done in developing Tier II/III cities as they evolve into viable IT-BPO service delivery locations. Efficiencies and the provision of public services – power, local transportation, security, etc. – are also critical for the development of this sector. With enhanced competition from other low-cost countries and the recessionary climate, the government could support growth through extending the tax incentives under the Software Technology Parks Scheme (STPI), remove procedural obstacles, that is, service tax refunds, taxation of software products and clarity around transfer pricing norms applicable to foreign companies. To help bridge the employable talent gap, it is important to increase the interaction and collaboration between business and academia, update curriculums, establish research labs and launch internship programmes. Trade bodies such as NASSCOM could enhance efforts towards information and data security, participate in public–private initiatives in technology-led development, and proactively promote industry–academia interaction to tackle the quality of education (*Business Standard*, 12 February 2009).

Another major factor that the industry fears is the backlash against outsourcing in the US. When Barack Obama was elected president, tax reforms were announced that were meant to penalise those companies that outsourced work out of the US. Although this had caused the ire of some top US corporations such as IBM, HP and Sun Microsystems, who had outsourced a majority of their work, experts said that the tax penalties would not compare with the cost arbitrage realised through outsourcing. 'A tax break can't compete with that kind of arbitrage,' said one US outsourcing expert (M. Srivastava, 2009). The US government also introduced an H-1B hiring ban for companies that received bailout money. In the background of seemingly unfavourable policies and a competitive global scenario beset with recessionary trends, it remains to be seen how the offshoring industry in India would maintain its growth and move further up the value chain.

5

Dr Reddy's Custom Pharmaceutical Services: A Tailor-Made Breakthrough Strategy in Pharma Offshoring?

Ananthi Rajayya

Overwhelmed by escalating pressures to reduce health care costs, elevated R&D budgets, diminishing numbers of new drugs as against leading blockbuster drugs going off-patent, coupled with numerous regulatory challenges in the West, global pharma companies were increasingly exploring low-cost options but highly skilled destinations for offshoring their pharmaceutical services in order to attain maximum efficiency and productivity. Consequently, in the race for survival, major pharma and biotech companies were seeking to keep hold of their drug discovery and portfolio management, while outsourcing their manufacturing and research processes, thus developing a cost-effective business model in the highly competitive arena and substantiating an ever-growing demand for contract research and contract manufacturing services.

Exploiting the increasing interest of global pharma companies in pharma offshoring in post-TRIPS scenario, Contract Research and Manufacturing Services (CRAMS), the fastest growing segment in the pharmaceutical industry, emerged as a huge opportunity for low-cost manufacturers. Captivated by the mammoth opportunities in CRAMS, many Indian pharma biggies who traditionally took the generic path until recently also customised their business models betting big on CRAMS. 'We are seeing a fundamental shift in Indian companies' approach from business driven research to an increasing focus on research-driven business,' said Utkarsh Palnitkar, Director of Ernst & Young India (*Pharmabiz*, 8 July 2004). With an estimated annual growth of 25 per cent, the Indian CRAMS sector was an attractive segment with a huge potential of US$20 billion CRAMS business, which was expected to reach US$31 billion by 2010 (Andheria, 2009). It also resulted in the emergence of innovation by service providers in offering research and manufacturing services. Some of them transformed from being a mere contract research player to a cost-effective, flexible and reliable one-stop-shop provider offering fully integrated and cost-effective pharmaceutical research and development, and custom manufacturing services to the innovator firms worldwide.

Dr Reddy's Laboratories Ltd (Dr Reddy's), one of the leading players in the Indian pharmaceutical industry and a leading generics player in the top pharma markets of the world, was also interested in moving up its value chain by creating a strategic unit called Custom Pharmaceutical Services (CPS). The unit offered tailor-made pharmaceutical solutions to innovator pharmaceutical companies right from the time a potential drug molecule was in the research stage, up until the product reached market. Through its CPS business unit, the company provided drug substance and drug product development, and manufacturing services on a proprietary basis.

With its strong network of strategic partners, niche technology-led acquisitions, high-level manufacturing services capabilities, a wide range of customised pharma ingredients and a track record of taking innovations to the market with greater speed, efficiency and lower capital expenditures, Dr Reddy's soon became the largest CPS player from India. It was expected that this pharmaceutical services offshoring model would ensure comfortable margins in the long run for the company, which was already struggling with pressures on earnings due to high R&D, legal and selling, and administrative costs. It was also perceived that Dr Reddy's, as a leading generic player, would undergo hardships owing to a shift in the Indian pharma industry in 2005 post-TRIPS (Trade Related Intellectual Property Rights) from 'Process Patent Regime' to 'Product Patent Regime' (Dhar & Gopakumar, 2006).

5.1 Company background

Dr Reddy's started as a manufacturer and supplier of raw materials for medicines, Active Pharmaceutical Ingredients (APIs) in 1984 and over the last two and a half decades the company has grown into a vertically integrated global pharmaceutical company with activities spanning the entire pharmaceutical value chain (Dr Reddy's, 2009a). From modest beginnings in Hyderabad, and established with an initial capital outlay of just INR 25 lakhs, the company has grown rapidly and gone global, with a strong presence in Europe, USA, Russia and China, earning a net revenue of INR 69.4 billion (US$1.37 billion) in 2008–9 (Reddy, 2009).

Founded by Dr Anji Reddy, the company initially supplied the API needs of the Indian market. Later the company became specialised in the manufacturing and selling of bulk drugs in India and abroad. It commenced operations with a single drug in a 60-tonne facility near Hyderabad. The first drug Methyldopa was shipped to West Germany. Dr Reddy's, which initially addressed the API needs of the Indian market as a supplier, underwent tremendous transformations following the 'Process Patent Regime' put in place by the Government of India in 1972 to promote and encourage the domestic health care industry in reverse engineering the drugs patented in the West (i.e. copy medicines patented abroad) to make cheap and affordable drugs for the general public. Prior to the process patent regime, MNCs dominated the Indian market and were ruling out the Indian pharmaceutical industry by selling drugs at a very high price. Consecutively, Indian pharma companies transformed their business model to shift from API manufacturing to generic players. The demand for reverse-engineered drugs arose not only in India but across the globe, which encouraged Dr Reddy's to focus on reverse engineering the molecules to produce generic/copycat versions of blockbuster drugs patented in the West.

In 1986, it transformed from a predominantly API-focused company to that of a formulation pharma company by starting its operation in branded formulations. It also obtained its first United States Food and Drug Administration (USFDA) approval for Ibuprofen API, the first generic product marketed under the 'Dr Reddy's' label in the US, following which it began exporting its formulations internationally. Within a year, the company launched Norilet, Dr Reddy's first recognised brand in India. However, it was Omez (Omezaprozole), an ulcer drug brand, that brought huge success to the company. Its superior process technology helped the company to launch Omez at a 50 per cent lower price compared to other brands in the Indian market.

Backed by the enormous demand for these copycat versions in the regulated as well as unregulated markets, in the mid-1990s, Dr Reddy's increased its scale of production and applied for getting approval from drug regulators to target Western generic markets, like the US and Europe, where the cost of the branded original drugs were exorbitant. Subsequently, the company filed a number of Abbreviated New Drug Applications (ANDA) with USFDA to get approval to market generics in the US. As of 31 March 2009, the company had filed 159 cumulative ANDAs (Reddy, 2009).

Recognising the growing demand for and significance of drug discovery and development, the company established a research foundation called Dr Reddy's Research Foundation in 1992. The foundation streamlined its research focus to innovative R&D and hired new scientists, especially Indian students studying abroad. Shifting its business model to drug discovery, it invested heavily in building R&D labs in India and overseas. Dr Reddy's became the first Indian pharma company to invest in its own R&D programmes. With strong financial support and research capabilities, the company commenced its R&D operations in 1993 and was actively involved in drug discovery research in various areas, including diabetes, cardiovascular disorders, metabolic disorders, cancer, inflammation and bacterial infection. The company was also keen to get into biotech drug discovery and development.

In 1994, Reddy started targeting the US generic market by building its state-of-the-art manufacturing facility funded through the GDR (Global Depositary Receipt) issue of US$48 million. In the same year, it also established its subsidiary Dr Reddy's Laboratories Inc. in New Jersey to cater to the growing demand for generic drugs in Western markets. It also set up an exclusive facility in the US to focus on manufacturing finished dosages for the regulated American market. Its rapid growth in the generic business was further fuelled by the introduction of the Para 4 filing law in 1997 which rewarded generic manufacturers for challenging existing patents instead of waiting for them to expire. Dr Reddy's was the first Indian pharmaceutical company to win a 180-day exclusivity for the generic brand Zocor. Its branded and unbranded generic products offered affordable alternatives to innovator brands, both directly and through key partnerships. Some of Dr Reddy's more famous generic brands in key markets are shown in Table 5.1.

As of 1999, the Indian pharmaceutical industry accounted for 70 per cent of the bulk drugs and 80 per cent of the formulations in the

Table 5.1 Dr Reddy's major global generic brands

North America	Germany	India	Russia
Simvastatin	Simvastatin	Omez	Omez
Sumatriptan AG	Alendron	Nise	Ciprolet
Fexofenadine	Oxycodon	Stamlo	Nise
Glimepiride	Omeprazol	Stamlo Beta	Enam
Oxaprozin	Tramadol	Atocor	Ketorol
Ondansetron	Ramipril & hcT	Razo	Exifine
Finasteride	Venlafaxin	Omez-DSR	Citrine
Meprobamate	Ibuprofen	Reditux	
Divalproex Spr. capsules	Ramipril	Mintop	
Ciprofloxacin	Gabapentin	Enam	
Tizanadine			

Source: Dr Reddy's.

country, making India one of the few countries in the world achieving self-sufficiency in drug production (Grace, 2004). While the pharma side of Dr Reddy's was fine-tuning its generic business strategy, it also concentrated more on its in-house R&D and drug discovery. Within three years of commencement of its R&D operations, in 1997, the company out-licensed an anti-diabetic molecule, DRF 2593 (Balaglitazone) to Novo Nordisk, a Danish pharma major, thereby earning the distinction of becoming the first Indian pharmaceutical company to out-license an original molecule. The following year, Dr Reddy's lab came up with another superior lead molecule in the same category called Ragaglitazone, which was also out-licensed to Nova Nordisk.

To speed up its R&D process and expand the drug-discovery segment, the company launched a research and discovery unit, Reddy US Therapeutics, in Atlanta, Georgia in 1999. The laboratory carried out research in the biochemical, molecular biological and chemical segments. Through setting up its research centre in the US, the company could easily understand the disease mechanism and provide access to latest technologies and talent that complemented the company's existing skill set.

With its immense success in API, branded formulations and generic business, Dr Reddy's became the first pharmaceutical company from Asia Pacific (outside Japan) to be listed on the New York Stock

Exchange in 2001. The company's diversified portfolio of businesses fuelled by the industry's move towards greater consolidation through mergers and acquisitions, prompted it look for an overseas acquisition. In March 2002, Dr Reddy's acquired BMS Laboratories and its wholly owned subsidiary Meridian Healthcare, for EUR€14.81 million. The capability of these companies to deal in oral solids, liquids and packaging with state-of-the-art manufacturing facilities in the UK was expected to contribute further to Dr Reddy's success in the overseas market. In 2004, its acquisition of Trigenesis Therapeutics Ltd, one of the specialists in the dermatology segment gave the company access to drug delivery technology platforms. In March 2006, the company acquired Betapharm, Germany's fourth largest generics pharmaceutical company, from 3i for EUR€480 million. The acquisition of Betapharm was regarded as one of the largest-ever foreign acquisitions by an Indian pharmaceutical company. It was expected that this acquisition would help Dr Reddy's to emerge as one of the leading generic players in Europe.

Dr Reddy's continued its acquisition spree and in 2008, it acquired BASF's pharmaceutical contract manufacturing business and related facility in Shreveport, Louisiana. During the same period, it took over Dowpharma Small Molecules business from Dow Chemical, UK and Italy-based Jet Generici. With mounting competitive and cost pressures, Dr Reddy's entered into multiple long-term agreements with leading pharma companies for research and development, joint development and the marketing and commercialisation of drugs. Some of the companies with which it had agreements were Leiner Health Products of USA, Pliva of Croatia, Rheoscience A/S of Denmark, Euro Drug Lab of the Netherlands, and ClinTec International and Argenta Discovery Ltd of the UK. In line with these agreements, Dr Reddy's and the innovator firms collaboratively completed the stage of clinical trials and drug development. They then shared the commercial rights to market the developed drugs in various regions.

In the post-Intellectual Property Rights era, the pharmaceutical industry was increasingly becoming competitive as most of the companies worldwide were trying to focus on drug discovery due to the large number of patent expirations, decreasing R&D productivity and the high costs of drug development. With a view to provide greater flexibility and lessen the risk involved in drug discovery and development, many of the Indian pharma companies spun off their discovery operations. They strongly believed that generics and innovation were two totally different businesses, with different time frames, certainty profiles and investments. Creation of a separate entity would be the innovative way to mitigate the risk as the success ratio in drug discovery was very low. They demerged their drug discovery operation into a separate entity, with the intention of reducing risk and attracting venture capitalists.

In light of this, Dr Reddy's ambition of securing a spot among the world's top innovation-led pharma companies resulted in the formation of India's first integrated drug development company, Perlecan Pharma Private Limited (Perlecan), in 2005 with an equity capital commitment of US$52.5 million from India's leading venture capital investors, Citigroup Venture Capital International Growth Partnership Mauritius Limited (Citigroup Venture) and ICICI Venture funds management company (ICICI Venture) (Dr Reddy's, 2005). Perlecan was established to engage in clinical development and out-licensing of New Chemical Entities (NCE) assets, the first step in the process of drug development.

Remarking on the creation of Perlecan, Dr Anji Reddy, Chairman of Dr Reddy's, said:

> These are exciting times for Indian pharmaceutical companies and we are pleased to announce the formation of India's first integrated drug development company. The formation of Perlecan acts as a precursor to many more exciting partnerships in the area of drug discovery and development for the Indian pharmaceutical industry. We have made significant progress in the last decade in building a strong drug discovery platform and look forward to further building on this foundation to realise Perlecan Pharma's potential. This partnership marks an important milestone for the Company and will put Dr Reddy's at the forefront of drug discovery and development over the next decade. We are pleased to welcome the involvement of Citigroup Venture and ICICI Venture, who bring important skills and experience to the new company. We value their support and confidence in future potential of Perlecan.
>
> Dr Reddy's (2005)

It was expected that Perlecan would provide Dr Reddy's drug discovery programme a model to rapidly advance its existing as well as future NCE assets through Phase II trials and seek out-licensing, co-development or joint commercialisation opportunities, thereby enhancing the value of the pipeline (Dr Reddy's, 2005). As part of this drug discovery programme, on 27 March 2006 Dr Reddy's transferred all titles and rights, including the development and commercialisation rights of its own four NCE assets, to Perlecan. Besides its own NCEs, Perlecan was also developing molecules in collaboration with Rheoscience and ClinTec International. In 2006, Dr Reddy's was the first Indian pharmaceutical company to report revenues over US$1 billion.

However, in July 2008, Dr Reddy's bought back the 43 per cent stake in Perlecan from ICICI and Citigroup following failures of some of the NCEs developed. Consequently, Perlecan became a 99.99 per cent subsidiary of the company with effect from 31 July 2008.

Over 25 years since its inception in 1984, Dr Reddy's continues its efforts to provide affordable and innovative medicines to patients across the world, either directly through its global generics business or indirectly through its pharmaceutical services business. Its strategy is to position itself as a global, vertically integrated company offering a wide portfolio of businesses: APIs, generics, branded formulations, biologics, specialty pharmaceuticals, custom pharmaceutical services and discovery research.

As of March 2009, the company had a presence in more than 40 countries with more than 160 products marketed in Europe, and over 200 branded formulations marketed in the rest of the world. The company has focused on markets in America, Europe, India and Russia. This portfolio was complemented by more than 100 US Drug Master Files (DMFs). Some of the world-renowned companies with whom the Dr Reddy's has entered into partnership and transacted with include Novo Nordisk, Novartis, Merck, GlaxoSmithKline, and Roche.

Despite its vertically integrated business model which provides a portfolio of services across the globe, the increasing legal and R&D costs on account of patent challenges and new drug discovery initiatives, a huge jump in selling and administration costs due to increased marketing costs as a result of new products launched in India and abroad, forced the company to declare a loss in 2008–9. Dr Reddy's net loss was INR 5168 million in 2008–9, versus a net profit of INR 3836 million in 2007–8.

5.2 Dr Reddy's Custom Pharmaceutical Services (CPS)

One of the major stumbling blocks for global innovators opting for low-cost options for their pharma services was fear of loss of patent protection arising due to the frequent transfer of pharma services projects from one service provider to another, looking for different processes and development. This happened mainly due to the inability of the service providers to set up a one-stop-shop offering a range of services, from contract research, clinical research to contract manufacturing. Innovators also had to struggle when hunting for service providers in niche segments like central lab services, preclinical safety assessment, toxicology, medicinal chemistry, chiral chemistry and custom synthesis. This had resulted in the delaying of projects, thereby increasing the research and development costs of innovators and generic firms instead of cost savings. In the US and Europe, the cost involved in introducing a new drug to the market was anywhere between US$0.5–1 billion, and took at least ten to 15 years. Approximately 50–60 per cent of the cost spent was only towards clinical development. Thus, there was an ever-growing demand for firms offering a complete range of services spanning across the new drug development processes.

Exploiting the increasing demand for versatile service providers in pharma offshoring, Dr Reddy's ventured into the CPS space in 2001 by creating a CPS segment to cater to the strategic outsourcing needs of innovators worldwide (Harachand, 2009). The move into the CPS space was envisioned by G. V. Prasad, managing director and CEO, and the person widely credited as the architect of Dr Reddy's successful global generics strategy. He saw the evolution of Dr Reddy's from a mid-sized pharmaceutical company into a globally respected pharmaceutical major, with the CPS segment as a highly regarded and strategic unit which would provide a complete range of services that were necessary to take pharma companies' innovations to market with more speed, efficiency and lower capital expenditures.

Since its inception, it has been one of the fastest growing segments in Dr Reddy's portfolio of businesses due to its innovativeness in catering to the needs of innovators and generic formulators by combining its service and generic expertise to offer custom-made pharma solutions in the challenging times facing the pharma industry. Dr Reddy's vision of providing affordable and innovative medicines to patients across the world, either directly through its global generics business or indirectly through its pharma services business further prompted its pharma offshoring services segment.

Understanding the need for highly specialised research laboratories to strengthen its portfolio of business segments, especially the research and development processes, Dr Reddy's had invested heavily in setting up R&D facilities across the globe. CPS executed cost-effective and time-sensitive projects for its customers, providing current good manufacturing practice (cGMP)-compliant products manufactured in USFDA-inspected and ISO-certified facilities. For instance, Dr Reddy's analytical R&D, a department which was involved in the analysis of drug substances and products at various stages of development and validation and characterisation and structure elucidation of NCEs, was facilitated by multiple, fully staffed dedicated analytical laboratories.

For the company's process R&D and scale up, there are two dedicated, state-of-the-art Technology Development Centres (TDCs) in Hyderabad, India. TDCs' 21 well-resourced synthetic organic chemistry laboratories are used to serve the needs in the chemical development of molecules. It also has a cGMP Kilo Lab/Pilot Plant for scale-up and early clinical material, with a Class 100,000 clean room and Class 100,000 cGMP cytotoxic suite for toxicology and early clinical material, besides a chemical and hazard evaluation laboratory.

As one of the important core businesses, Pharma's API business accounted for 40 per cent of the company's total sales. India played an important part in the global API market and was ranked fourth in the world in terms of API output with a CAGR of 18.81 per cent. The key API producers, including Ranbaxy, Dr Reddy, Cipla Ltd, Cadila Healthcare and Matrix, produce more than 400 types of API and around 10,000 kinds of reagents, satisfying over 90 per cent of Indian domestic demand. According to the Tata Strategic Management Group, it was expected that Indian API export would enjoy a rapid growth in the coming years and increase to US$12.75 billion in 2012 from US$3.75 billion in 2007 (India APIs Industry Report, April 2009). Utilising the rapid growth in the API segment, Dr Reddy's had filed 55 DMFs in 2008–9. Of these, 21 were filed in the US, five in Canada, 19 in Europe and ten in other countries. As of 31 March 2009 there were cumulative filings of 351 DMFs, with 148 in the US.

Six high-performance multi-ton API production facilities are dedicated for API segments in India. Further, Dr Reddy's US$59 million acquisition of Roche's API business at the state-of-the-art manufacturing site in Cuvernavaca, Mexico has helped the pharma major to jump-start plans for its own CPS business. Besides manufacturing APIs such as Naproxen and Naproxen Sodium, the Mexico facility pioneered the synthesis of steroids used in the pharmaceutical and veterinary industries since 1967.

The acquisition has added unique steroid manufacturing capabilities to the domestic pharma giant, thereby helping the company to emerge as a leading player in the CPS business. The key customers include Roche and other innovator companies based in North America and Europe. In addition, the acquisition has also added expertise in complex chemical syntheses and cryogenic reactions. The acquired facility, with installed production capacity of 3350 tons, consists of seven manufacturing bays of which two were dedicated to steroid capabilities. All facilities are USFDA-inspected, ISO-certified and cGMP-compliant facilities. Unique steroid manufacturing capabilities, coupled with its strengths in process chemistry and world-class dedicated technology development centres has laid a strong foundation to drive the next wave of growth in the CPS business. It is expected that the acquisition would provide an opportunity for the company's CPS business to grow ten-fold to US$100 million in the coming years and further de-risk the company's strategy which was focused on drug discovery and generics.

Dr Reddy's oral solid manufacturing segment has engaged in converting dosage forms into finished packs, manufacturing and supplying tablets/hard gelatin capsules to three pilot plants dedicated to oral solids manufacturing. Its high potency contract manufacturing has the ability to handle cytotoxic oral solids and cytotoxic injectables.

Backed up by well-equipped manufacturing and R&D facilities; an experienced team consisting of more than 950 research scientists, 1400 process engineers, 8000 project coordinators and business development staff; flexibility to produce and deliver suitable quantities of NCEs with scales ranging from initial gram to kilogramme to multi-ton requirements, Dr Reddy's CPS unit serves as a single-point contract offering tailor-made pharma solutions to global innovator pharmaceutical companies and emerges as a trusted supplier of value-added services.

Generally, the R&D process in the development of new medicines takes several years and encompassed a wide range of expertise and skills. Discovering and bringing one new drug to the market typically costs a pharma company millions of dollars and takes an average of ten to 15 years. Through its CPS business unit, Dr Reddy could facilitate innovators worldwide right from the time a potential drug molecule was in the research stage until the product reached market.

CPS' competitive advantage lay in its unique and novel business model which combined the company's expertise and experience in generics, and API business with innovators' service expertise to offer a full spectrum of services: dosage development capabilities from preformulation, formulation development, cGMP clinical batch manufacturing, scale up, registration batch manufacturing to commercial manufacturing. The focus of CPS is to leverage on skills in process development, analytical development, formulation development and cGMP manufacture which allows for speed and flexibility in the supply of both small-scale clinical trial quantities and commercial-scale quantities.

Dr Reddy's expertise and experience in maintaining a wide portfolio of businesses, competitive pricing and end-to-end services has led the company to become the largest CPS player from India and a partner of choice to innovators, offering top-end technical expertise, tailor-made pharma solutions with a track record of bringing innovations to the market quickly, efficiently and economically. Its systematic way of providing services starts from its project evaluation. Each and every project taken up by the company undergoes a thorough investigation and an in-depth survey which helps to identify the needs and scope of the project. Through the evaluation process, the CPS unit guarantees that each custom synthesis project is thoroughly evaluated and accepted by all departments concerned, before a final proposal is made to the customer.

The company's objective is to become the preferred partner for innovator companies by providing a complete range of services that is necessary to take their innovations to market with more speed, efficiency and lower capital expenditures. Dr Reddy's specialised project management teams consist of experienced CPS chemists and engineers, who work closely with their clients from initiation to closure and provide high-quality, cost-efficient products and services rapidly. Heavy investment in world-class software, hardware and communication channels help support each functional team to move up the projects seamlessly to completion, with the aim of meeting the customer's expectations.

Quality assurance and quality control play a crucial role in client satisfaction at Dr Reddy's. The company ensures that quality is maintained at every stage through active engagement at all stages of the process, from the development of the API to the submission of finished dosage dossiers to the regulatory agencies. With a view to streamline new product development processes, Dr Reddy's has implemented Project 'Rachna' using Microsoft Accelerator for Six Sigma. This is expected to help the company in taking key decisions to launch the right products in the market at the appropriate time and to quickly identify opportunities and develop new products catering to those requirements.

Further, the company's acquisitions spree in this segment in recent years is expected to advance its growth in the CPS business. Through its acquisition in 2008 of Dow Pharma's Small Molecule business associated with its Mirfield and Cambridge sites in the UK, Dr Reddy's has even greater access to customer contracts and relationships, associated API products, process technology and know-how and technology licensing rights. The company also took over the existing work force as part of the acquisition. This acquisition resulted in technology-related synergies for Dr Reddy's PSAI and gave it access to an experienced research and development team (Dr Reddy, 2009b).

The acquisition of BASF Corporation's pharmaceuticals contract manufacturing business and its manufacturing facility in Shreveport, Louisiana in USA enabled Dr Reddy's to access BASF's resources, including customer- and product-related intangibles, trademarks as well as the Shreveport manufacturing facility. Jet Generici Srl, a company acquired in 2008 engaged in the sale of generic finished dosages in Italy. This acquisition resulted in Dr Reddy's gaining entry into the Italian market, acquiring product-related intangibles, a strong employee workforce and access to customers.

5.3 Road ahead

Dr Reddy's was looking at revamping its business model in pharmaceutical services offshoring to beat competitive pressures in generic drug manufacturing. As part of the strategy, in September 2008,

Dr Reddy's combined its CPS and API segment to form a new segment called Pharmaceutical Services and Active Ingredients (PSAI) (Joseph, 2008). The company expected that PSAI would contribute over 25–30 per cent of its revenues in the next couple of years. Abhijit Mukherjee, president of Dr Reddy's PSAI commented, 'At present, it contributes only 10% to our revenues, which is $1.25 billion. The environment for pharmaceutical outsourcing is favourable as innovators look to reduce costs and increase the speed of research. We would also look at acquisitions in this area' (Golikeri, 2008). Through the revamped model, Dr Reddy's expected to deal better with increasing competitive pressures in the generics business, thereby generating new streams of revenue in order to continue to grow and to ensure comfortable margins in the long run. However, Mukherjee, opined that 'although the profit margins are better, pipeline services are not highly scalable and result in a less predictable revenue stream, especially in current times, compared with the large-scale commercial services' (Thayer, 2009). He further commented that there was 'limited opportunity for long-term collaborations with emerging drug firms. Although we do a lot of early-stage work, it is not very easy to imagine that one would remain a partner until launch. The journey is very long, and the chances of those assets making it to the end are increasingly lower these days' (Thayer, 2009).

According to Jeffrey M. Evans, president of Rondaxe Pharma, 'the only way the one-stop-shop business model becomes sustainable is if and when the service providers can become aligned with the goals of the innovators' (Thayer, 2009). Further, India's imminent shift from process patent regime to product patent regime implemented in India in the post-TRIPS scenario perceived that Indian firms would no longer be able to duplicate the latest Western medicines that would result in cutting off their major source of revenues. On the other hand, there was a silver lining following the amendments that it would attract huge contract R&D and therefore multinationals would prefer to open their R&D centres in India. Hence it became essential for prominent Indian firms like Dr Reddy's, Ranbaxy, Wockhardt and Lupin Laboratories to seek out new opportunities such as engaging in their own drug-discovery research, promoting manufacturing facilities and carrying out clinical trials.

With a view to mitigate the huge losses incurred in 2008–9, Dr Reddy's engaged in restructuring its business model. As part of its restructuring plan, the company closed its Atlanta research facility in the US, one of the first R&D facilities of the company outside India. Another major restructuring plan was the absorption of its drug discovery operations in Hyderabad by Aurigene, a wholly owned independent subsidiary of the company, with effect from 1 July 2009 (*The Financial Express*, 22 May 2009). As part of this, the discovery research resources, employees, facilities and infrastructure would transition into being resources of Aurigene.

One of the buzzwords in R&D offshoring was Drug Discovery and Development Support Services (DDDSS) under which R&D, once considered as the sacred cow, something companies would never share with other companies, was outsourced by global pharma giants, since developing in-house capabilities to cover such intermittent needs was considered economically unfeasible. Migration of drug R&D from the West to emerging countries became irrefutable as many of the processes involved in drug discovery were time-consuming, laborious and involved huge R&D costs.

Expecting a major shift in drug discovery offshoring, many leading pharma companies which maintained a portfolio of generics and CRAMS started prioritising company-wide R&D spending and placed emphasis on drug discovery activities that could have a significant impact on near-term earnings. Dr Reddy's also took part in this major shift. In custom pharmaceutical services segment, it focused more on transiting its business model from contract research service to contract manufacturing. Out of the projected US$2.5 billion market by 2012, contract manufacturing accounted for the maximum share of the total manufacturing outsourcing business in India and was expected to cross US$900 million by 2010, followed by clinical trials which was growing at the compound annual growth rate of 31 per cent and was set to become a US$608 million industry by 2012 (*The Hindu Business Line*, 30 September 2009). With over US$70 billion worth of drugs expected to go off patent in the US, the world's largest pharma market, in the near future, Dr Reddy's was keen on moving up its chain into streamlining its in-house and collaborative research and drug discovery, to seek opportunities in drug discovery offshoring. 'The Indian generic industry is well positioned to benefit from the structural and macro-economic changes affecting the healthcare industry globally,' according to a report on the Indian generic industry (*The Economic Times*, 2 August 2009).

On 15 June 2009, UK based GlaxoSmithKline plc (GSK), the world's second largest pharmaceutical company, announced an agreement with Dr Reddy's to develop and market selected products across an extensive number of emerging markets, excluding India (Dr Reddy's, 2009c). As part of the agreement, GSK would gain access to Dr Reddy's rich and diverse portfolio and future pipeline of more than 100 branded pharmaceuticals in the fast-growing therapeutic segments such as cardiovascular, diabetes, oncology, gastroenterology and pain management. The products would be manufactured by Dr Reddy's and licensed and supplied to GSK in various emerging markets such as Africa, the Middle East, Latin America and Asia-Pacific excluding India. Revenues will be reported by GSK and will be shared with Dr Reddy's as per agreed terms. In certain markets products will be co-marketed by Dr Reddy's and GSK.

Commenting on the collaboration, G. V. Prasad, vice-chairman and CEO of Dr Reddy's said, 'We are extremely pleased to combine forces with GSK, a global leader, to fully realize the potential of our strengths in technology, product development and manufacturing across a range of high growth emerging markets. We hope to take our purpose of providing affordable and innovative medicines to a much wider population through this partnership' (Dr Reddy's, 2009c).

6
Legal Process Outsourcing Opportunity and Cobra Legal Solutions

Sathyanarayanan Ramachandran

Bangalore has long been known as India's information technology hub, and just a five-hour drive away from the city is Chennai, the southern metropolis of India and the capital of the state of Tamil Nadu. It was an unusually extended summer morning for 32-year-old Sakthivel Venkatraman, the managing director of operations of the New York headquartered Cobra Legal Solutions LLC (CLS), one of the leading legal process outsourcing service providers. Sakthivel was busy streamlining the operations in India and spearheaded the expansion plans. He had just moved to their new facility at Ascendas International Technology Park and was pondering over various strategic opportunities and challenges of the promising new business landscape. The increasing acceptance of outsourcing legal processes in the West had pumped up the growth rate of this new opportunity and also invited several new players to enter. Nevertheless, it also threw up unique challenges for the service providers in India and especially for the fledgling ten-year-old company. According to Sakthivel, the way the Company started was an interesting story in itself, since CLS did not originate in USA or India's major business or law schools.

6.1 Company background

In 1999, John and Becky Douglas tragically lost their daughter, Amber. When John and Becky went through Amber's personal effects, they discovered that Amber had been sending a portion of her college allowance to an orphanage in India. As a tribute to Amber, Becky later travelled to India. She was so moved by the needs of the people that Becky organised a group of friends and started a charitable organisation called Rising Star Outreach. Rising Star started providing medical, educational and economic assistance to the leprosy-affected families and their children in the settlements of Tamil Nadu. Becky met and later partnered with Padma Venkatraman, the daughter of a former President of India. Together, Becky and Padma established micro-lending programmes in addition to ongoing assistance programmes in Tamil Nadu and extended their reach to the fishing villages affected by the 2004 tsunami. In 2007 Rising Star relocated its hostel and school to a new 13.5 acre facility near Chennai, with the aim of housing 300 children and educating 800 children (Cobra Legal Solutions, 2009).

As a result of Rising Star, Becky brought the issues of leprosy-affected people to the attention of her friends in the US. One Cantwell Muckenfuss went to India to work with the children from these settlements to complete his service obligation for high school. His mother, Angela Lancaster, joined him. Angela and Cantwell shared Becky's love for the children. They also, through Rising Star, became good friends with Mohan Subramanyam and Meena Mohan, his wife. Mohan was the CEO of Kumaran Systems, an information technology services company based in Chennai with offices in the US and Canada. Mohan and Meena's daughters, Manju and Swathi, also volunteered at Rising Star. Through these relationships, the group came together in an enterprise centred on children.

Contemporaneously, John, Mohan and Chuck, Cantwell's father, began discussing globalisation and India's increasingly important role in the world economy. This was just as *The New York Times* columnist Thomas Friedman wrote: 'The World is Flat'. Each recognised the tremendous opportunities associated with pairing the needs of corporate law departments with the intellect and talent of Indian-trained lawyers using modern technology. After extensive analysis of the needs of US corporations and law departments and resources in India, the core approach of CLS was developed: combine world-class processes, procedures and controls, excellent and motivated Indian attorneys and US-trained personnel on both sides of the ocean.

Each of CLS' founding group was convinced that the CLS model provided the framework for reshaping the legal profession dramatically. They understood the importance of excellence and the need for delivering that quality at an attractive price. Each believed that the CLS model met a compelling need in a manner that assured quality and timeliness and in 2007 CLS, a Delaware limited liability company, was formed.

The management team was headed by Jeff Dickerson, the CEO. He was a practicing lawyer and was responsible for CLS' overall operation and financial management and strategic direction. Jeff Isenberg was the MD of technology and operations in the US and was primarily responsible for the company's technology, information-management systems, communications, data storage, as well as operational processes. Kevin M. Clark was the MD of litigation in India who was primarily responsible for managing the litigation operations and support services of CLS in the country. He was also responsible for the oversight and management of the India-based attorney team. Sakthivel Venkatraman was the MD of operations in India and was primarily responsible for managing the day-to-day operations and support services of CLS in India. A. Angela Lancaster, as chief administrator officer, assisted with CLS' financial, corporate, human resource and other operational functions.

6.2 Legal process outsourcing

Legal process outsourcing (LPO) is a value-added business process outsourcing service which has invited considerable interest among various law firms and corporations in developed countries due to some inherent cost and value advantage. Compared to a BPO, LPO is a specialist knowledge-driven activity as one moved up the value chain. Two major types of LPOs include captive units and third-party service providers. Captive units are basically service units for a single parent law firm or corporation whereas third-party service providers offer their services to a multitude of clients across the globe. Various services offered by LPOs include contract management, legal document review, preparing deposition summaries, litigation document management, legal research and analysis, patent drafting, legal auditing and contract drafting.

The service spectrum ranges from low value-added data entry functions to high value-added services like legal research. The cost savings are up to 30 per cent in lower-end jobs like data entry and transcription, and around 50–70 per cent for value-added services like patent searches (Jha, 2009). Successful LPOs have an effective marketing team in their client countries and an efficient delivery team at home. According to a KPMG report, the first-level document review as a cost component in the total litigation cost ranges from 58–90 per cent. Thus, by outsourcing this to lower-cost countries, law firms could make substantial savings (Olivas & Dolan, 2006). Apart from the cost, another major advantage in outsourcing to countries like India is the reduction of turnaround time due to the difference in time zones.

CLS mainly focuses on document review and management solutions, and litigation technology consulting by using both offshore and onshore legal talent. This included responsive and privilege review of documents in response to litigation or governmental inquiries, including issue tagging and production of detailed privilege logs; preliminary review of documents for pre-litigation assessments and internal investigations; institutional document management; due diligence review of internal documents in connection with business transactions; Hart-Scott-Rodino, a US antitrust law, compliance review for 4(c) filing and second requests, and; Sarbanes-Oxley compliance review of internal documents, which was legislation for new or enhanced standards for all US public company boards, management and public accounting firms.

CLS provides litigation technology consulting services to assist clients in managing the entire range of e-discovery and case management needs, from the beginning stages of collection, to processing, hosting and document review. CLS also has capabilities in providing contract management, legal research, case summaries, deposition summaries and other litigation support services.

6.2.1 The LPO industry

According to IDC India, a global intelligence firm, India's domestic BPO market is expected to touch US$6.82 billion by 2013. The industry recorded revenues of US$1.62 billion in 2008 and was expected to grow at a CAGR of 33.3 per cent. As the industry matured, there was a gradual shift towards value-added non-voice processes like LPO.

A Forrester Research study pegged the 2008 value of the LPO market in India at US$80 million and predicted that it could reach US$4 billion by 2015, thereby providing employment potential for 80,000 jobs (Parnami, 2007). As per a ValueNotes study, the recessionary impact on the global legal industry has had a cascading effect on the Indian legal process outsourcing industry. There seemed to be a temporary slowdown with the growth rate plummeting from a CAGR of 40 per cent in 2003–7 to 16 per cent for 2008–9. The industry recorded revenues of US$320 million in 2008 and was expected to reach US$440 million by 2010 (ValueNotes, November 2009).

The 2008 recession in the US had become a new business opportunity for the LPOs. An increase in home loan foreclosures had added tempo to the LPO business. A report in *Businessworld* stated that 'according to RealtyTrac, which publishes the national database of foreclosures, 279,561 US properties got default notices, auction sale notices and bank repossessions in October 2008 alone, which is one in every 452 US housing units. The foreclosure numbers have increased 5% compared to September 2008 and 25% compared to October 2007. There are 1.5 million properties across 2,200 counties and 50 states in the US' (Ganesh, 2008). According to Forrester, 35,000 lawyer jobs would shift offshore by 2010 and about 79,000 by 2015 (Sachitanand, 2009).

6.2.2 The India advantage

In the sphere of outsourcing, India scores well with its demographic advantage and also due to its proven track record in the IT/IT-enabled services industry for the past two decades Table 6.1. Also, the availability of talent at a lower cost compared to the developed world is a major factor in driving the industry. In the US, if junior associates charges an hourly rate of US$150–275, the same job could be handled by an Indian attorney for an hourly rate of just US$15–25 (Loranger, 2008).

Further, since Indian law is very similar to British Common Law, Indian law graduates find it relatively easy to grasp the nuances of the legal system in the UK and US. Around 80,000 law graduates who are fluent in English come out of the annals of law institutions in India annually.

The main factors that are favourable for LPOs in India include: difference in time zones helping to reduce the turnaround time for clients; the government understanding the employment potential of this industry and providing various infrastructure facilities, incentives and tax holidays; a well-developed telecom infrastructure;

availability of 1.8 million lawyers (Kshama, 2007) and the government concerned about data security issues.

6.2.3 The India inhibitors

With all the rosy opportunities, there were several inhibiting factors with respect to outsourcing services from India. The major restraining issues to overcome were related to data security and the perception on the quality of work. There were some incidents of data theft in Indian BPOs, which had added fuel to this fire (*The Times of India*, 11 November 2009).

Taking cognizance of this issue the National Association of Software and Services Companies (NASSCOM) had taken several measures to address the concern. Among the measures take was the establishment of the Data Security Council of India (DSCI) as a self-regulatory organisation (SRO) (NASSCOM, 2009b). Along with the DSCI, the government was also trying to plug the holes in the legal system by adding more stringent rules in the Information Technology Act. The DSCI suggested implementing several best practices and privacy practices (P. Srivastava, 2009).

By May 2009, just 3 per cent of UK and US firms had outsourced their back-office work to India. A positive sign was that some of the top UK law firms like Linklaters, SJ Berwin, Freshfields Bruckhaus Deringer and CMS Cameron McKenna were exploring legal process outsourcing options. Firms like Allen & Overy were already outsourcing the litigation document review to India (Sadowski, 2009). Other contenders competing for these opportunities were LPOs from countries like South Africa and the Philippines.

In order to tackle some of the security issues, CLS requires US and Indian employees and supporting contractors to sign agreements mandating confidentiality and security of client information. Cobra's agreements with its clients allow for parties to resolve any disputes in the US pursuant to the commercial arbitration rules of the American Arbitration Association. CLS has state-of-the-art infrastructure including a world-class data centre, hosting customer data of the highest degree of sensitivity and of a restricted nature. The centre conforms to the highest and most stringent security measures. The Tier I facility offers both physical protection, including biometric access controls, state-of-the-art surveillance systems, 24/7 security guards and network protection – including multiple firewalls and password protection.

For added data security, attorney reviewers are neither allowed to print from their workstations nor allowed to copy anything to a removable media device like a CD or thumb drive. In addition, USBs, CDs and thumb drives are not permitted in the workplace. CLS also restricts attorney access to external email, and access to the Cobra's facility is with a cardkey system and security checkpoints.

Clients normally have their data hosted in the US. If there are data privacy issues involved with the collection of data in a country with strict privacy laws, clients could have their data hosted in the UK or the country where the data is collected, depending on the legal judgement of the attorneys overseeing e-discovery or e-disclosure.

Another area of concern was the question of downstream risks in offshoring the outsourcing process. According to the Black Book of Outsourcing 2009, countries in Central and Eastern Europe, Latin America and China would reap from India's temporary and permanent risks. Also, the report classified offshore locations as safest and riskiest based on various parameters, including anti-corruption enforcement, pollution, terrorist targets, etc. Many of the Indian cities listed in the report appeared on the risky side (Brown & Wilson, 2009).

Though, this was not a company-specific issue for CLS, Sakthivel had been pondering over the strategic implications with the CEO. This was where the role of the government and industry bodies like the Confederation of Indian Industry (CII), NASSCOM, National Association of Legal Offshoring Companies (NALOC) and Business Process Industry Association of India (BPIAI) had become very important in tackling these issues and eliminating, what were considered, overhyped fears.

In the US markets, the question of ethics came into the picture as the US government regulations made it mandatory that only lawyers who were licensed in the US could provide legal advice on American Law (Kshama, 2007). This led to several constraints for Indian LPOs. According to Sakthivel, the American Bar Associations argued that working with offshore attorneys was ethical, when appropriately managed. ABA Ethics Opinion 08-451 stated that US lawyers were free to outsource legal work, including to lawyers or non-lawyers outside the country, if they protected confidential information and ensured that the service providers were competent, suitably trained and properly supervised.

6.3 CLS service delivery

CLS has around 80 qualified attorneys in their Chennai facility who handle various legal processes. They are well trained in US laws and depending on the project, customised training is also given from time to time. The MD of litigation manages the entire work flow in the Chennai facility. This is backed up by a robust technology backbone that gives instant access to client documents through web-hosted document review platforms in a secure environment. Further, all the project-related communications such as decision logs, changes in the protocol, updates and outstanding queries are documented to facilitate clear communication.

There are stringent multi-tiered quality control measures which include pre-review of documents, sampling, specialised quality control teams, coding conflicts reports, specialised searches with close monitoring on site by US-trained lawyers, led by the MD of litigation in Chennai. Conference calls are held on a daily basis with client attorneys to communicate work status. On a need basis, CLS also integrates the preferred quality control measures into their regular project-specific operations.

6.3.1 The cost advantage

The primary advantage of outsourcing at large is the inherent labour arbitrage between India and developed countries like the US and UK. But, according to Sakthivel, CLS goes one step further in bringing the cost further down with excellent quality control processes and project management techniques. The clients are provided with real-time reports on the costs incurred and CLS also assists their clients in managing the vendor relationships. Some of the striking highlights of the pricing structure include a bouquet of pricing plans, hourly rates, price-per-GB and per-document-pricing plans; no overtime, equipment or facilities charges; per-document-pricing plan provides a fixed-cost alternative to hourly rates; fees billed are reconciled to equal the lowest of the applicable billing methods (especially during multiple billing cycles).

Sakthivel also explained a unique 'Least Cost Pricing Plan' followed by CLS. Under the Least Cost Pricing Plan, projects are quoted with three rates: an hourly rate, a per gigabyte rate and a per document rate. The final amount invoiced to the customer is determined by whichever pricing method (hourly, per gigabyte or per document) produces the lowest cost.

According to Sakthivel, this is very useful for the client because, when choosing a document review company, accurate cost comparisons could be difficult. Performance metrics from previous projects are no guarantee that your project would run efficiently. A low hourly rate is no bargain if the rate of review slowed to a crawl, or when multiple layers of more expensive management time are added on. Cobra's Least Cost Pricing Plan thus reduces the client's headache in a single stroke. Taking these advantages into account, CLS needed to have an effective marketing and branding strategy in place, firstly towards potential clients and secondly, towards potential employees in order to attract talent.

6.3.2 Talent and human resources

The LPO industry is purely driven by knowledge workers. An industry boom would result in a talent crunch and it was imperative for the LPOs to take up right strategies not only to attract talent but also to invest in capacity-building strategies. Another issue was the attrition rate, which according to an estimate was as high as 70 per cent (Rebello, 2008).

A survey conducted by ValueNotes in 2008 stated that Indian law graduates least preferred LPO as a career choice. There was a strong perception that it was just another monotonous BPO job (*Live Mint*, 15 December 2008). This was a serious revelation when the industry was betting on the annual output of 80,000 lawyers from law colleges. Apart from this, leaving out a handful of Tier I institutions, Indian law graduates predominantly come through a rote-learning process rather than a Socratic method, which was necessary for higher-end legal analysis jobs. Hence, for customised LPO skills, extensive training was needed for the sector to thrive. The training needed to concentrate on global orientation, international laws and practices, culture, language and accent.

The Indira Gandhi National Open University (IGNOU) stepped in along with Rainmaker, a Mumbai-based legal talent management and training company, to fill this gap with its new one-year course on legal process outsourcing (Post-Graduate Diploma in Legal Process Outsourcing or PGDLPO) to train lawyers and final year law students. The two-semester programme has four components that trains candidates on legal knowledge and skills, industry awareness and preparedness, technology and legal ethics, and communication: Professional English Proficiency (PEP); Virtual Intelligence Methods (VIM); Legal Education and Proficiency (LEAP); and Skills, Personal Effectiveness and Enterprise Development (SPEED).

IGNOU has partnered with leading LPOs for internships as part of this programme and the programme was developed in consultation with leading LPO players, legal luminaries and legal academicians. The programme is delivered through e-learning in IGNOU's 61 regional centres across the country. The cost of the programme is INR 18,000 (approximately US$391) and the first batch saw an enrolment of 200 candidates.

At the organisational level, to mitigate this important skill-set bottleneck, CLS has an initial 12-week training programme that focused on US federal rules of civil procedure with a focus on Discovery; E-Discovery basics using the EDRM Model to ensure best practices; litigation application training (Case Central); document review training on the dummy database; and introduction to US legal research and writing (Bluebook, citations, sources and style).

Apart from this initial training there are other ongoing training programmes which centre on introduction to document review software tools (e.g. Case Central, Documatrix, Discovery Radar, DocHunter, Concordance, Ringtail, Summation and ADI); daily reading and comprehension exercises based on current events in the US legal and business fields (*The Wall Street Journal*, *The New York Times* and *The Washington Post*); training in US grammar and idioms; and dummy database training and simulation of real-time scenarios.

Cobra's Chennai facility has 60 attorneys, ten support staff and a capacity for 200 attendees. As the public training programmes, like PGDLPO, percolates into the system, the expenditure on internal training would come down considerably and firms could concentrate only on client-specific training programmes.

6.4 CLS' major competitors

As the sector grows rapidly, lot of companies are jumping onto the bandwagon. There are more than 100 vendors in the LPO field in varying sizes ranging from pure-play legal service providers to major BPOs and IT companies. Compared to a margin of 12–15 per cent in the BPO space, LPOs offer a margin of around 40 per cent with fewer workforces (Parnami, 2009). This has attracted even big players like Infosys, Wipro and HCL into the sector. Soon the industry has been expected to have a shakeout and get into a consolidation mode. Many big players have also been on the lookout to acquire smaller players. The major players include Mindcrest, Pangea3, Clutch Group, Quislex, SDD Global and Integreon.

6.4.1 Mindcrest

Established in Chicago in 2001, Mindcrest is the largest and fastest-growing legal support services company with more than 700 lawyers in Chicago, New York, San Francisco, Washington DC, Mumbai and Pune. Mindcrest was selected by the Association of Corporate Counsel (ACC) as the legal process outsourcing company in its ACC Alliance Program. As part of the programme, ACC members receive a 10 per cent discount on all Mindcrest litigation services projects exceeding US$50,000 (Mindcrest, 2009).

6.4.2 Pangea3

With hundreds of employees globally, Pangea3 is the established leader in legal outsourcing services to international corporations and law firms. Headquartered in New York City and Mumbai, Pangea3 was founded in 2004 and has since grown to become one of the largest legal process outsourcing companies globally (Pangea3, 2009).

6.4.3 Clutch Group

Clutch Group is a leading global provider of legal support solutions, with integrated operations throughout the US and India. They serve corporate legal departments and major law firms in the following areas: discovery solutions, compliance review, contract administration and legal research services. Clutch Group has US offices in Washington, New York, Chicago, Cleveland, as well as an office in Bangalore, India, where they operate a world-class, state-of-the-art legal support facility. Clutch Group was rated the number one LPO company worldwide in 2008 by the Brown-Wilson Group, publisher of *The Black Book of Outsourcing* (Clutch Group, 2009).

6.4.4 Quislex

Quislex is a New York-headquartered company founded in 2004. It is one of the first companies to get ISO/IEC 27001:2005 certification for data security and information security management system. Quislex opened their second facility with a capacity of 200 in Hyderabad, India (Quislex, 2009).

6.4.5 SDD Global

With offices in Mysore, Bangalore, New York and London, SDD Global's legal outsourcing work involves high-end legal research, analysis and drafting, as well as patent and immigration visa services. It is the only provider of outsourced legal services in India managed by a US law firm, the New York-based SmithDehn LLP (SDD Global, 2009).

6.4.6 Integreon

Promoted by Philippines-based Ayala, Integreon focuses exclusively on outsourcing complex, knowledge-intensive tasks. Its clientele includes two of the three largest global law firms, AmLaw 100, 100 UK law firms, seven of the ten largest investment banks, several top-tier private equity firms, hedge funds and many *Fortune 100* and FTSE 100 corporations. Integreon has been in business for a decade and has 2000 employees. Recently Integreon acquired Grail Research, the captive research unit of the Monitor group with delivery centres in China and South Africa (Integreon, 2009).

6.5 Conclusions

There is a new growing opportunity for an emerging economy like India in legal offshoring due to the cost and value arbitrage. As a promising company, Cobra Legal Solution's managing director of India operations, Sakthivel, analysed the strategic and operational issues facing the young company in the promising business domain of legal process outsourcing. When looking at the industry environment, it is important for CLS to analyse the issues of selecting an offshore destination from a client's point of view and to analyse the various strategic issues, including the business environment, marketing, branding, service delivery and talent management, from the service provider's point of view.

With the mushrooming of service providers and a rapid growth rate, the industry is clearly in an expansion phase and is witnessing increased competition. This calls for increased investment and many non-LPO players from the IT and ITES sectors aspire for inorganic growth by acquiring niche players. Also, the entry barriers are relatively high as the industry requires unique skill sets and different processes. This could slow down the growth of even established players from the non-LPO sector. With the advent of new competition, it is time for existing service providers like Cobra to create their own niche brand, to aggressively market themselves to potential clients and to also attract talent for the long term. This calls for a distinct brand-building function to create a global identity for the CLS brand – one that would be embraced by both employees and clients.

To conclude, the LPO opportunities for India and Cobra Legal Solutions are tremendous. But, there are many macro-level issues to be addressed. At the macro-level, Cobra should work with industry associations in contributing to capacity building, talent augmentation, country perception and national competitiveness. At the firm level, the company should focus on services marketing and brand management issues.

7
eInfochips: Product, Delivery and Service Differentiation

Vrajlal K. Sapovadia

eInfochips, an Indian IT company based in Ahmedabad, is an internet protocol (IP)-driven product development services company conducting global business activities in electronics design services and providing solutions in chip design, embedded systems and application software. The service and manufacturing capabilities of the company extends from specification-to-silicon-to-system to Chip/ASIC/SoC design and verification, physical design, board design, embedded system designs and testing, IP core and application development.

7.1 Company background

Recognising the synergy between Indian engineering talent and the requirements of the US market, Pratul Shroff founded eInfochips in 1995 with an initial capital of INR 5 million and just one design engineer, working out of his home in Ahmedabad. Shroff grew the capital by splitting the stock and converting some of the cash reserves into equity capital. From its modest beginnings, the company grew to employ over 600 engineers across its four design centres in Ahmedabad and two design centres in Pune. The company also has offices in the US, including centres in Sunnyvale, Austin, Chicago, Boston and New Jersey and it also started operations in Japan in 2007 by opening a Japan subsidiary – eInfochips KK. For other locations the company has appointed representatives and dealers in Taiwan, Korea, Israel, UK and the US who represent the products and services of the company in the marketplace. eInfochips soon became a leading provider of cutting-edge ASIC design services, embedded systems solutions and IP cores, with offshore development centres in India.

Pratul Shroff holds a bachelor's degree in Electronics Engineering from the Birla Institute of Technology & Science (BITS) and a master's degree in Computer Engineering from Cornell. He also studied management at the Indian Institute of Management (IIM), Ahmedabad. On completion of his studies, Shroff spent over ten years in Silicon Valley working for Intel and Daisy Systems. At Intel, he was a member of the 80,816 Intel Processor design team, the fountainhead of the PC era. As founding engineer at Daisy Systems, he helped the company reach US$125 million in sales and 1200 employees within five years of its founding. Shroff also co-founded Contech Systems in India before he embarked on a new venture, eInfochips.

Shroff's vision was to make eInfochips an innovative technology company that would have a transformational impact on society by creating leaders and generating stakeholder value. To attain this, eInfochips vision was to differentiate its product, delivery and service to the client. At the company's inauguration of its Bangalore centre in 2007, Shroff as CEO of eInfochips noted the company's success in establishing itself as a leading electronic design services provider by virtue of its expertise, healthy customer list, skilled workforce and seasoned management team, but also highlighted that eInfochips was at an inflection point where the company needed to leverage resources to aggressively expand revenue, accounts, geographies and infrastructure.

The Government of Gujarat promoted the venture company Gujarat Venture Finance Limited (GVFL), which was set up to assist young, first-generation technocrats to create innovative products and services. And one of those promoted was the young technocrat entrepreneur, Pratul Shroff, whose company received an initial financial support of US$400,000 from GVFL to establish a manufacturing unit. The company was also substantially internally funded. Thereafter, eInfochips obtained first and second round of funding from GVFL's SME Technology Venture Fund. GVFL helped specifically in drawing the strategy roadmap for the company and with its extensive network brought experts onto the company's board. It also assisted in showcasing the company at various state-level events and encouraged it to implement good corporate governance practices and to streamline its systems and processes. This helped eInfochips in its initial pace of growth and established a strong foundation for growth. GVFL takes pride in its investment and eInfochips is listed as one of its success stories on its website (GVFL, 2009). In 1997, 1998 and 1999 the Software Technology Parks of India for Gujarat Jurisdiction awarded the company 'Best Software Exporter'.

7.2 Design, differentiation and expansion

By 2001, eInfochips had made its own space in the Gujarat industrial world as a progressive industrial house but it had also made an impact on the global IT business. Indian companies had begun to make large profits from exporting chip design services. Shroff said that 'In 2001 the chip designing sector was valued at about US$130 million. Taking the opportunities and challenges, in 2003–04, the company achieved revenue of INR 190 million, and targeted revenues of INR 1.38 billion by five years' time. Strategically, the company brings differentiation by delivery of the product, using "Unique Amplified Offshoring" delivery model, which increases the effectiveness of services, that offers combinational advantage of both offshore, on-site modes' (eInfochips, 2009).

eInfochips has five design centres in India and three sales offices in the US, where the company maintains 30 to 40 engineers who serve as the link between the customer and the design team. The company considers these engineers 'product champions' and essential to its business, as they bridge the gaps – communication, cultural, temporal and geographic – between the US-based customer and the India-based design team. The company differentiates services to the clients by demonstrating the ability to address the entire spectrum of solutions. To ensure and meet the ever-changing demands of the technology industry, eInfochips provides a special kind of technical and management training known as 'Chipmates' and a compulsory year-long 'Life Skills' training on teamwork, time management, communication, and how to deal with cultural gaps and attitude. In 2004, the company was selected to operate the Qlogic Design Centre while the CEO, Shroff, received an AMA Outstanding IT Entrepreneur of the Year Award 2004.

To expand in terms of product, customer and geography, the company planned to enter into the Asia-Pacific market and open a Centre of Excellence for Chip Design and Product Design. With an investment of US$1 million spread over a campus of 15,000 square feet and capable of housing 170 engineers, eInfochips opened a third design centre in Ahmedabad in April 2006. By then eInfochips had achieved over 150 complex chip design and verification and system design projects for customers across the globe. Concurrently, eInfochips announced that it would contribute 1 per cent of its annual corporate profit for community initiatives and social causes, and contributed INR 251,000 to Gujarat Government's 'Kanya Kelavani Nidhi'. The company has also been working closely with 'Visamo Kids' and 'Sharda Trust'. The fund is dedicated for the education of girls and orphans.

eInfochips attained its vision by differentiating product, delivery and service to clients. The company identified six differentiating strategic factors: customer first – exceed expectations; deep-rooted services and solutions culture; operational excellence, proven delivery models and global experience; high degree of resource and technology scalability; business stability and quality leadership; and 3 per cent revenue investment in technical and non-technical training of the employees.

To achieve customer's business objectives of cost competitiveness and shorter time-to-market and to leverage, the company introduced the 'Amplified Outsourcing Model', for operational excellence and uncompromising commitment to quality. eInfochips opened its fourth design centre in Ahmedabad in 2006, which occupied nearly a 1000 square metre space and housed more than 140 engineers. The new design centre focused on complex chip design and verification, and product design services for consumer multimedia applications. On the opening of the centre, Shroff observed, 'We are witnessing unprecedented growth in design services market. Our endeavour is to continuously seek new ways to add value and benefits to our customers. eInfochips fosters an open, transparent and nurturing work culture. The company has preserved a Silicon Valley like entrepreneurial environment with a flat organization, and innovative technologies.'

To cater to the ever-changing needs of the market and equip employees with expertise, eInfochips conducts various training programmes in developing soft skills and technical matters. Skills which are highlighted in the training programmes are communication, business ethics, project management and leadership.

7.3 New service offerings

By the turn of the twenty-first century, Indian IT companies had started expanding their service offerings to provide a complete basket of services to their clients. These new services included IT consulting, testing, business process management and IT infrastructure services, which in a way allowed IT companies to de-risk their business from pricing pressures and enter into newer areas which provided them with higher growth and profitability. In 2005 eInfochips partnered with PolyVision to design an innovative visual communication tool, which won the CII award for 'Emerging ICT Enterprise in Gujarat'. To keep pace with the rapidly growing sector, the company set up a second design centre in Pune in 2006 and targeted 80 per cent growth in 2006–7. The new design centre was spread over an area of 10,000 square feet and housed more than 75 engineers, doubling eInfochips' headcount in Pune. In the financial year 2005–6 eInfochips achieved a turnover of US$10.4 million. 'The new Pune Design Centre will house an embedded lab for developing reference designs for video surveillance and videoconferencing applications on DaVinci™ technology from Texas Instruments Incorporated (TI). In addition, the new centre will include a centre of excellence for Vera and SystemVerilog based chip verification,' stated Tapan Joshi, VP of marketing at eInfochips.

The design centre at Pune executes projects for QLogic and develops new embedded tools and testing suites for the Tensilica processor. The company provides solutions and services to leading technology companies like Qlogic, Texas Instruments, ATI, Synopsys, Ponico, Rambus, Cypress Semiconductor and Navionics. One area where eInfochips has differentiated their products is in the verification space. As the complexity of chips increased, so did the challenge of verification, which could easily consume 50 per cent of the total design cycle time. The company provides training to its employees in high-level verification languages such as Specman and Vera. eInfochips is a third-party network member and is one of only two TI Certified Software Integrators. The other differentiation is in delivery of the product, by using the unique Amplified Offshoring Model (AOM), which increases the effectiveness of services and offers the combinational advantage of both offshore and on-site modes.

7.3.1 Amplified Offshoring Model and quality focus

The benefits of the Amplified OffShoring Model is that the company takes ownership for delivery – not the client; domain knowledge competency is built, retained and expanded; there is a dedicated team over the entire duration of project; shadow resources are introduced to make sure the project is on schedule; there is the benefit of aggregated project management process and methodology; and it enables proactive planning avoiding last-minute scrambles (Fig 7.1).

At the forefront of AOM implementation was ennovate Technologies, the software division of eInfochips. It was involved in developing 'Thunder', a tool for enterprise collaboration and distance learning. One of the clients wanted to launch a prototype of the product at a trade show (InfoComm 2005) that was just two months away from the start of project. ennovate Technologies was provided with a concept specification and the challenge was to develop a working prototype in this short space of time. The key differentiator in this collaborative tool was that, unlike other conferencing systems, the

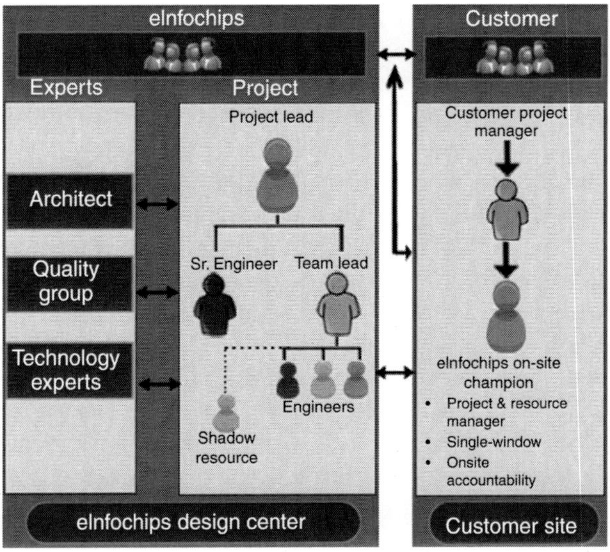

Figure 7.1 Amplified Offshoring Model
Source: eInfochips.

information data was retrieved and available to all attendees using virtual flipchart tool, scanner, real-time video and one-click publish feature. The client entrusted ennovate for a complete Product Lifecycle Management, including design, development of architecture and QA for the complete system. The overall achievement of the project was recognised when the company got into NASSCOM's 100 IT innovators 2007 list. The company invested heavily and expended great resources for market research, technology and service delivery.

The company's continuous process goal is to improve project execution and maintain a commitment to quality commitment, one that is implanted in products, services and processes at all levels and divisions of eInfochips. The company set up the Centralized Quality Management System (QMS) which consists of various procedures and standards (templates, forms, guidelines, tailoring guidelines and checklist). It is based on CMMi Level 3 and helps minimise the errors, defects and reworks, and at the same time continues to improve quality levels across the projects with respect to its domain and process standards. The company believes in continuous improvement and learning, therefore it has invested in training and workshops to make every employee an independent performer. Meeting the client's expectations is the focus of eInfochips and there is continual work on the technology and process improvement side for better performance and results.

7.4 Partners

eInfochips has built strategic relations with several organisations to create symbiotic relations. The company has been coordinating and cooperating with other companies when it found partnering as a means to grow. One such partnership is with Digilogue Communications, a digital brand communications service. The promoter of the public relation company Torque Communications and Digilogue Communications, Supriyo Gupta, explained the need for technological and financial investment from companies like eInfochips: 'We found increasingly a lot of the conventional stuff that we did were no longer relevant. People were no longer waiting for news to happen in the next day's newspaper and they were not even waiting for it to be broadcast on TV. They were getting it on their mobile phones and as email alerts.

The manner in which the news was happening was changing. The explosions of the social networking sites and blogs have changed the manner and flow of communication.'

As Verification Alliance Program Partners for Cadence, eInfochips has enabled the accelerated adoption of new technologies and improved the productivity of verification teams, leveraging years of experience and reusable verification IP. eInfochips has expertise on Specman Elite and offers design verification services, and consultation both on-site and offshore. It has also developed verification components eVC and uVC and is a member of Incisive® Plan-to-Closure Methodology Verification Alliance programme.

eInfochips has also partnered with Mentor Graphics' Questa Vanguard Program (QVP) which extends Mentor Graphics' range of design and verification technologies through partnerships with industry-leading companies. QVP partners provide verification-related tools and methods, verification IP, conversion services, training and consulting based on Mentor Graphics' Questa Verification Platform.

eInfochips is a Synopsys' SystemVerilog Catalyst Program Partner and its existing verification package has been extended to support SystemVerilog. This combined initiative enables customers to migrate from legacy environments to a VCS Natïve Testbench environment for up to five times faster verification performance. eInfochips is also a member of VMM Catalyst Program that is aimed at accelerating the widespread adoption of the industry-leading VMM verification methodology for SystemVerilog.

As a TI Third Party Network Member eInfochips works very closely with TI's technical and sales team for providing on-site and offshore consulting services in the areas of product development and project execution based on Texas Instruments' various DSP families. This offers the inherent advantages of low cost, high quality and faster turnaround to the customers. As a TI Third Party Authorized Software Provider (ASP), eInfochips provides and supports robust software codecs, ready-to-use TI application software and tested documented code. eInfochips has augmented TI ASP with its expertise in engineering services, application domain knowledge and understanding of TI's software products.

SIS Development, Inc. has partnered with eInfochips to provide full end-to-end product development at a fraction of the cost of internal development. Specialised wing-to-wing commercial OEM product development allows customised services based on a client's business model and specific needs. From product conceptualisation through product launch, SIS has implemented dependable processes and services, providing predictable results. SIS Development's services in partnership with eInfochips includes all aspects of product development, including market requirements definition, domestic project management, industry-specific expertise including business professional services, system design/architecture, design engineering, R&D, quick-start access to existing designs, compliance testing and product launch.

eInfochips is an ObjectVideo OEM (Original Equipment Manufacturer) partner and has collaborated with OV to deliver cost-effective, targeted, DSP-based, intelligent video solutions. ObjectVideo OnBoard has been integrated into eInfochips' TI DM642 reference design and DaVinci Rapid Prototyping Board.

eInfochips has helped jump-start development of projects with proven design and development expertise. It has designed and developed solutions for embedded systems, based on Windows platforms and is a member of the Microsoft Windows Embedded Partner program (WEP). The intent of the program is to enable WEP partners to bring their Windows-powered products to market faster.

7.5 Changing growth drivers

In terms of user industries, the banking, financial services and insurance (BFSI) and hi-tech/telecommunication industries remain the leading verticals for Indian IT companies. Together, these sectors account for around 58 per cent of the Indian IT-ITES exports. Though these verticals have good growth potential, other sectors such as manufacturing, airlines and transportation, retail, health care, and utilities are also emerging as promising segments for Indian IT companies. While the BFSI sector has the potential to provide large-sized contracts to IT companies, the manufacturing sector could also provide a large number of deals and projects to Indian players.

Many Indian software service companies are facing similar challenges, as with increased growth comes rising attrition rates. A 2007 McKinsey report stated that India would need an additional one million employees to join the IT-BPO workforce by 2010 in order to maintain its current market share. Managing attrition in the IT industry is considered extremely important since skilled professionals form the core of this knowledge-intensive industry. Apart from the loss of skill sets, the cost of recruitment and training is a huge investment for most IT firms. The attrition rate at eInfochips is approximately 15 per cent and so for the company to retain talent and promote employee creativity, eInfochips has implemented human resource policies that provide motivational and financial support, and promote research.

The industry has been changing and Pratul Shroff noted that in his business systems houses have been moving away from application-specific integrated circuits (ASICs) to field-programmable gate arrays (FPGAs). 'The costs of doing an ASIC have simply become too high for many designs,' he explained (Wilson, 2008). So in areas such as broadcast equipment, surveillance and health care, Shroff has seen large FPGAs displacing medium-sized ASICs. The transition has not been without its problems and Shroff observed that as the largest FPGAs come into use, placement and routing has become increasingly difficult. The old concepts of programmable logic, from cut-and-try design to push-button automated placement, are simply breaking down in the face of the growing complexity and the extremely high timing and power costs of even slightly inefficient routing (Wilson, 2008).

According to Shroff the thing that seems to help most with the placement and routing of these large FPGAs is to have a design team with cell-based back-end design experience. 'Standard-cell placement experience becomes vital on some of these projects,' said Shroff. There are some interesting economic implications to Shroff's observations. If the back-end flow in FPGA designs is becoming as complex and difficult as the back-end design for a cell-based ASIC, then the major savings in non-recurring engineering (NRE) has to come from other areas. The savings could come from front-end design, where the FPGA vendors have poured resources into raising the level of abstraction, employing pre-qualified IP and containing the entire flow in a single-user interface. Other savings could be found from the remarkable IP libraries assembled and supported by FPGA vendors, or they could come from the fact that FPGAs recover their manufacturing costs from their unit price (Wilson, 2008).

7.6 Key challenges for eInfochips

eInfochips' president and CEO, Pratul Shroff saw four main challenges facing the company. Firstly, the emergence of electronic products locally designed specifically for the Indian and regional markets. This would stimulate the development of product definition and architecture skills necessary for any product design activity. To overcome this challenge, eInfochips had to create a strong demand-pull with a strong electronic manufacturing base for the local market (Chakraborty, 2005). Secondly, electronic design services companies needed to move up the value chain and develop whole products in addition to the existing focus on engineering services. Currently, most technology companies are either the captive design centres of MNCs or third-party service providers with a few IPs. The third challenge was a lack of product engineering capabilities. This largely arose from the weak connections between design firms in India and Asian factories that put Indian companies at a disadvantage as compared to Taiwanese and Korean companies. eInfochips had to develop R&D capabilities to deliver value in the product chain. The fourth and final challenge as seen by Shroff was the ability to generate the skilled manpower supply to support growth. Global semiconductor design was moving increasingly to India due to the availability of skilled engineers with experience in hardware and software. Any skills shortage would hamper growth for eInfochips. It was estimated that the Indian engineering colleges trained only about 250 to 300 VLSI engineers annually, while it was projected that chip design services would require 20,000 additional engineers in the coming years (Chakraborty, 2005). In response to this potential industry crisis, eInfochips initiated industry–academic collaborations, including course and curriculum design, faculty training and student-placement assistance.

7.7 Key developments for eInfochips

eInfochips has been persistent in developing its products and services by aapplying the *Kaizen* principle of focusing on continual improvement. One of eInfochips product developments was the introduction of Digital Video Processing Board-High Definition (DVPB-HD) for Texas Instruments' (TI's) DaVinci Technology in the last quarter of 2008. DVPB-HD is a digital media processor based on DaVinci Technology and provides all commonly used video system peripheral interfaces. This allows original equipment manufacturers and original design manufacturers to go to market by reducing their hardware design cycle. The board is targeted at various applications that need video encoding and/or decoding capabilities, such as videoconferencing, surveillance, digital media adaptor and medical-imaging devices. DVPB-HD is also bundled with a boot-loader and software utilities which allows customers to develop or re-target their applications to the DVPB-HD.

In June 2009 eInfochips announced VMM-enabled verification IP for the Synopsys DesignWare(R) Verification IP Alliance Program and availability of Verification Methodology Manual (VMM). The eInfochips VIP has also been added to the Synopsys DesignWare(R) Verification IP Alliance Program. The Alliance program gives designers access to a broader range of VMM-enabled verification IP, which complements the DesignWare Verification IP portfolio. Synopsys selected and qualified eInfochips for the Alliance program because of its extensive experience in verification, VMM methodology and verification IP development. eInfochips' VMM-enabled MIPI CSI-2, DSI and HSI, and SDIO VIP products are based on the layered architecture of object-oriented programming that allows coverage-driven verification suitable for verifying transmitter and receiver with either of them as the design-under-test (DUT). Earlier in March 2009, eInfochips announced the availability of two reference designs featuring Marvell Sheeva CPU Technology and availability of two Marvell(R) Kirkwood Series(TM) 88F6281 SoC-based reference designs, the OpenRD-Base and the OpenRD-Client. This cost-effective, high-performance, low-power reference designs offer developers a versatile, open platform to evaluate and develop software for solutions targeted at various market segments. eInfochips and Marvell also made available the complete hardware and software design information to the developer community on their websites, including the schematics, layout, bill of materials, uBoot and Linux support package and file system. Customers and original equipment manufacturers (OEMs) could build their products based on these open platforms directly or with modifications tailored to their specific needs.

7.8 Emerging markets

The Indian IT industry has witnessed several issues and challenges affecting its growth, despite the fact that demand conditions have been optimistic. Therefore, it is important for companies to adopt best practices to address those issues in order to sustain the current growth momentum. Several large and mid-sized companies have taken innovative measures to try and address some of the challenges: for example, in light of the continuous rupee appreciation against the US dollar, Indian companies are keen to expand their businesses to other emerging markets.

In terms of geographical contribution, the US continues to remain the key market for Indian IT companies, accounting for 67.2 per cent of the total IT-ITES exports from India. However, Europe is also emerging as an important market for the Indian IT industry, considering the fact that the share of exports to Europe from India increased from 22.2 per cent in FY2003 to 25.1 per cent in FY2007. Indian companies are increasingly enlarging their footprint in countries of Latin America, Eastern Europe and Asia-Pacific region. Mergers and acquisitions have been one of the quickest routes for Indian companies to enhance their presence in European markets.

Pratul Shroff has employed a two-pronged growth strategy for eInfochips. First is taking the company into new markets in Asia-Pacific, including Japan, Korea and Taiwan, which are all large centres of electronic manufacturing and chip consumers. The company was keen to tap these markets and win new customers. A beginning has already been made in 2006 when eInfochips set up a Japanese subsidiary, eInfochips KK. The second growth strategy is to capture larger value from the entire spec-to-silicon-to-system value chain by offering customers a full service range of comprehensive electronic design services. By combining access to Pune's existing talent pool and academic infrastructure for developing strong engineering resources, the company felt that Pune was an ideal location for advancing eInfochips expansion plan. eInfochips already had four state-of-the-art design centres in Ahmedabad and Pune, and employed over 600 design engineers across the locations. In 2007 the Pune centre contributed 15 per cent to eInfochips' overall turnover. The year 2008 was fruitful for eInfochips, as the company launched 7th Reference

Design for the video industry and received the GESIA award for 'The Best Innovation by ICT Company' and the 'Texas Instrument Award' for outstanding work on DaVinci™ Technology.

7.9 Conclusions

eInfochips maximises its value chain by offering innovative products and services to its customers through motivated and highly trained employees, and commits resources in a timely manner to build production capacity. The company endeavours to continuously seek new ways to add value and benefits to its partners. eInfochips has attained its vision by differentiating electronics and IT products, and in the delivery of products and services to clients through innovation and equitable value distribution among the stakeholders. While the company's CAGR was 18 per cent there is still room for improvement by expanding the product line horizontally and vertically. eInfochips' top and bottom line is on a growth trajectory since its establishment and it has a well-set system in place coupled with market reputation and internal talent pool, for that trend to continue. The Indian IT sector is predicted to remain a growth engine in the coming years and hence eInfochips could leverage on its core competency.

Bibliography

Andheria, Mahalaxmi (2009) 'Indian pharma and new patent regime', 24 August. Available at http://www.pharmainfo.net/og/pharmindia/indian-pharma-and-new-patent-regime

Bloomberg Businessweek (5 June 2006) 'Big Blue shift'. Available at http://www.businessweek.com/magazine/content/06_23/b3987093.htm

Bloomberg Businessweek (3 September 2007) 'A red-hot Big Blue in India'. Available at http://www.businessweek.com/magazine/content/07_36/b4048052.htm

Business Standard (12 February 2009) 'Outsourcing must to remain competitive'. Available at http://www.business-standard.com/india/news/outsourcing-must-to-remain-competitive/348786/

Business Wire (2 September 2002) 'Wipro increases stake in Spectramind eServices Private Ltd'. Available at http://findarticles.com/p/articles/mi_m0EIN/is_2002_Sept_2/ai_90962701/

Businessworld (26 January 2008) 'On new legs'. Available at http://epi.nasscom.in/Nasscom/templates/NormalPage.aspx?id=55673

Brown, Douglas and Scott Wilson (2009) *The Black Book of Outsourcing*, revised edition, Hoboken, NJ: John Wiley & Sons.

Chakraborty, Pradeep (2005) 'Design hub challenges before India'. *EDN Asia*, 20 December. Available at http://www.einfochips.com/news/20051220-edn-asia.pdf

Click, Rick L. and Thomas L. Deuning (2005) *Business Process Outsourcing: The Competitive Advantage*, Hoboken, NJ: Wiley.

Clutch Group (2009) Company information available at http://www.clutchgroup.com

Cobra Legal Solutions (2009). All information unless otherwise stated was taken from the company website and approved by the company. Available at http://www.cobralegalsolutions.com/

De, Rajneesh and Goutam Das (2006) 'Dataquest's story on GE', 2 September. Available at http://www.infics.com/news/news180.asp

Dhar, Biswajit and K. M. Gopakumar (2006) 'Post-2005 TRIPS scenario in patent protection in the pharmaceutical sector: The case of the generic pharmaceutical industry in India', November. Available at http://www.iprsonline.org/unctadictsd/docs/Dhar%20Indian%20Pharma%20November06.pdf

Dr Reddy's (2005) 'Dr. Reddy's announces the formation of Perlecan Pharma. Perlecan Pharma raises USD 52.5 million as initial equity capital. Perlecan Pharma: India's First Integrated Drug Development Company'. Press release, 28 September. Available at http://www.drreddys.com/media/press-releases.html#

Dr Reddy's (2009a) 'About Dr Reddy's'. Available at http://www.drreddys.com/aboutus/about-drreddys.html

Dr Reddy's (2009b) 'Annual Report 2008–2009'. Available at http://www.drreddys.com/investors/pdf/annualreport2009.pdf

Dr Reddy's (2009c) 'Dr. Reddy's announces strategic alliance with GSK for Emerging Markets', 15 June 2009. Available at http://www.drreddys.com/media/popups/jun15_2009.html

e-Infochips (2009) All quotes and company information are taken from the company website unless otherwise stated. Available at http://www.einfochips.com/

'Evaluserve: The next big opportunity – moving up the value chain – from BPO to KPO', Evalueserve Report, 13 July 2004. Available at http://www.asiapacificdirect.com.au/big_opportunity_moving_up_the_value_chain%20-%20from_bpo_to_kpo.pdf

Ganesh, Venkatesh (2008) 'Outsourcing: Blessing in disguise'. *Businessworld*, 16–22 December.

Ganguly, Dibeyendu (2007) 'GE's global showpiece at Bangalore'. *The Economic Times*, 21 September. Available at http://economictimes.indiatimes.com/features/corporate-dossier/ges-global-showpiece-at-bangalore/articleshow/2388474.cms

GE (2009) 'Thomas Edison & GE'. Available at http://www.ge.com/company/history/edison.html

A. T. Kearney Study (2009) 'Geography of Offshoring is Shifting', 18 May. Available at http://www.atkearney.com/index.php/News-media/geography-of-offshoring-is-shifting.html

Golikeri, Priyanka (2008) 'Crams sees bounty in slump'. *DNA Money*, 14 July. Available at http://www.sify.com/finance/crams-sees-bounty-in-slump-news-default-jegrX4gcdcb.html

Govindarajan, Vijay (2009) 'Winning micro customers in mega markets'. GE Reports, 11 March. Available at http://www.gereports.com/winning-micro-customers-in-mega-markets/

Grace, Cherie (2004) 'The effect of changing intellectual property on pharmaceutical industry prospects in India and China'. DFID Health Systems Resource Centre, June. Available at http://www.who.int/hiv/amds/Grace2China.pdf

GVFL (2009) 'Success stories'. Available at http://www.gvfl.com/successstories.html

Hamm, Steve (2006) 'IBM wakes up to India's skills'. *Bloomberg Businessweek*, 5 June. Available at http://www.businessweek.com/magazine/content/06_23/b3987098.htm

Harachand, S. (2009) 'The emerging second wave', 8 October. Available at http://www.contractpharma.com/issues/2009-10/view_india-report/the-emerging-second-wave/

IBMa (2009) 'Research areas'. Available at http://www-07.ibm.com/in/research/researcharea.html

IBMb (2009) 'Blue Gene'. Available at http://domino.research.ibm.com/comm/research_projects.nsf/pages/bluegene.index.html

'India Active Pharmaceutical Ingredients (APIs) Industry Report 2008–2009' (April 2009). Available at http://www.Reportlinker.com/p0118594/India-Active-Pharmaceutical-Ingredients-APIs-Industry-Report-2008-2009

India Brand Equity Foundation (2005) 'R and D, The New Sunshine Sector', February. Available at http://www.ibef.org/artdisplay.aspx?cat_id=391&art_id=5519

Integreon (2009) Company information available at http://www.integreon.com

Rattanani, Jagdish (2007) 'Customer care: Rising star', 1 December. Available at http://www.infosys.com/BPO-services/total-telecom.pdf

Jayashankar, Mitu (2007) 'The leader's way: How GE safeguards vital information'. *The Economic Times*, 2 June. Available at http://articles.economictimes.indiatimes.com/2007-06-02/news/28476867_1_ip-jfwtc-employees

Jha, Ambrish (2009) 'LPO – Legal Outsourcing Business is on the Upswing'. *Dare*, January. Available at http://cobralegalsolutions.com/pdf/Top%2010%20LPO's.pdf

Joseph, Lison (2008) 'Dr Reddy's new model to focus on niche services'. *Live Mint*, 11 September. Available at http://www.livemint.com/2008/09/10231453/Dr-Reddy8217s-new-model-tc.html

Kaur, Gagandeep (2008) 'Platform BPO: Platform for growth'. *Voice & Data*, 4 December. Available at http://voicendata.ciol.com/content/bporbit/bpo/108120402.asp

Khanna, Ajay. (2006) 'Tapping the knowledge goldmine'. *The Financial Express*, 30 November. Available at http://www.financialexpress.com/news/tapping-the-knowledge-goldmine/185306/0

Kim, W. Chan and Renée Mauborgne (2005) *Blue Ocean Strategy: How to Create Uncontested Market Space and Make The Competition Irrelevant*, Boston, MA: Harvard Business School Press.

Knowledge@Wharton (2003) 'The little start-up that could: A conversation with Raman Roy, Father of Indian BPO', 4 June. Available at http://knowledge.wharton.upenn.edu/article.cfm?articleid=794

Knowledge@Wharton (2005) 'R&D in India: The Curtain Rises, the Play has Begun', 21 November. Available at http://knowledge.wharton.upenn.edu/article.cfm?articleid=1278

Kripalani, Manjeet (2007) 'IBM: Star of India'. *Bloomberg Businessweek*, 23 August. Available at http://www.businessweek.com/globalbiz/content/aug2007/gb20070823_174101.htm

Krishnakumar, Dhanya (2008a) 'Indian IT's Fourth Wave'. *Businessworld*, 26 January. Available at http://epi.nasscom.in/Nasscom/templates/NormalPage.aspx?id=55675

Krishnakumar, Dhanya (2008b) 'Blinkered Vision'. *Businessworld*, 14 August.

Kshama, N. (2007) 'Legal process outsourcing – A perspective'. Manthan Services. Available at http://www.manthanlegal.com/documents/LegalProcessOutsourcingPerspectivePaper.pdf

Kulkarni, Vishwanath (2009) 'Lighting up R&D at GE'. *The Hindu Business Line*, 7 September. Available at http://www thehindubusinessline.com/todays-paper/tp-eworld/article1084469.ece

Kundu, Kunal Kumar (2004) 'India, the world's R&D hot spot'. *Asia Times*, 18 August. Available at http://www.atimes.com/atimes/South_Asia/FH18Df01.html

Legal Process Outsourcing (16 October 2009) 'A comparison of four most popular LPO destinations'. Available at http://lpowatch.blogspot.com/2009/10/comparison-of-4-most-popular-lpo_7365.html

Live Mint (15 December 2008) 'LPO firms find it difficult to attract talent'. Available at http://www.livemint.com/2008/12/15172105/LPO-firms-find-it-difficult-to.html

Loranger, Guy (2008) 'Affects of technology and economics to law firms: Columbia to Calcutta'. *South Carolina Lawyers Weekly*, 28 July.

McIntyre, Douglas A. (2009) 'IBM and the rebirth of outsourcing'. *Time*, 26 March. Available at http://www.time.com/time/business/article/0,8599,1887779,00.html

Mahanta, Vinod (2009) 'India to play key role in GE's operation disruption'. *The Economic Times*, 30 September. Available at http://articles.economictimes.indiatimes.com/2009-09-30/news/27658657_1_jeffrey-immelt-indian-market-india-and-china

Mindcrest (2009) Company information available at http://www.mindcrest.com

Mishra, Pankaj (2009) 'IBM local outsourcing pie to be 50% by 2010'. *The Economic Times* 10 February. Available at http://articles.economictimes.indiatimes.com/2009-02-10/news/27640414_1_outsourcing-contracts-ibm-s-india-software-labs-innovative-solutions

Mitra, Raja M. (2007) 'India's Emergence as a Global R&D Center'. ITPS Swedish Institute for Growth Policy Studies. Available at http://www.dudebin.com/library/indiafrad.pdf

Narayan, Suchitra (2009) 'Asia/Pacific business process outsourcing 2009–2013 forecast and analysis, 2009'. Available at www.IDC.com

NASSCOM (2008) 'Strategic Review 2008: The IT-BPO Sector in India', New Delhi, February.

NASSCOM (2009a) 'Indian IT-BPO Industry 2009: NASSCOM Analysis', February. Available at http://www.scribd.com/doc/54953143/IT-Industry-Factsheet-Mar-2009

NASSCOM (2009b) 'BPO Forum, Security', 5 November. Available at http://epi.nasscom.in/Nasscom/templates/NormalPage.aspx?id=58180

'NASSCOM-BCG Innovation Report 2007: Unleashing the Innovative Power of Indian IT-ITES' (July 2007) Available at www.nasscom.org

NASSCOM-McKinsey (2005) 'Extending India's Leadership in the Global IT and BPO Industries', New Delhi.

Olivas, Dario and Michael Dolan (2006) 'Legal process outsourcing of first level document review'. *Sourcingmag Insights*, 18 September. Available at http://www.sourcingmag.com/content/c060918a.asp

Pangea3 (2009) Company information available at http://www.pangea3.com

Parnami, Pankaj (2007) 'Calibrating competence for professional excellence', *KPO Consultants*. Available at http://www.icsi.edu/WebModules/Programmes/35NC/35NCPilot%20Papers.pdf

Parnami, Pankaj (2009) 'Marriages in LPO industry'. *KPO Consultants*. Available at http://www.kpoconsultants.com/index.php?option=com_content&v

iew=article&id=49:32nd-all-assam-chess-championship-2009&catid=2:events&Itemid=15

Patel, Nitisha (2007) 'Offshoring lifecycle of GE Capital International Services'. Available at http://www.watsonwyatt.com/pubs/horizons/media/2007_12/pdfs/watson_wyatt_horizons_offshoring_p14-16.pdf

Pharmabiz (8 July 2004) 'India to become global pharma outsourcing hub: E&Y Report'. Available at http://www.pharmabiz.com/article/detnews.asp?articleid=22872&sectionid=50

Quislex (2009) Company information available at http://www.quislex.com

Rai, Saritha (2006) 'I.B.M. will triple investment in India in next 3 years'. *The New York Times*, 7 June. Available at http://www.nytimes.com/2006/06/07/business/worldbusiness/07blue.html

Ramana, K. V. (2009) 'Outsourcing 3.0: GE'll manufacture here now'. *DNA*, 17 September. Available at http://www.dnaindia.com/money/report_outsourcing-3-0-ge-ll-manufacture-here-now_1290850

Rangela, Renu (2009) 'Growing together'. *Quality India*, Vol. III No. 1, May. Available at http://www.qcin.org/nbqp/qualityindia/Vol-3-No1/retaining.htm

Rebello, Snehal (2008) 'LPO: Q&A with bigwig'. *Hindustan Times*, 31 March. Available at http://www.hindustantimes.com/News-Feed/HT-Story/LPO-Q-amp-A-with-bigwig/Article1-294845.aspx

Reddy, K. Anji (2009) 'Chairman's speech'. *Moneycontrol*, March. Available at http://www.moneycontrol.com/annual-report/drreddyslaboratories/chairmans-speech/DRL

Sachitanand, Rahul (2008a) 'GE's innovation hub'. *Business Today*, 6 April. Available at http://businesstoday.intoday.in/story/ges-innovation-hub/1/1786.html

Sachitanand, Rahul (2008b) 'IBM's discovery of India'. *Business Today*, 15 October. Available at http://businesstoday.intoday.in/story/ibm%E2%80%99s-discovery-of-india/1/3223.html

Sachitanand, Rahul (2009) 'Wanted: Legal eagles'. *Business Today*, 17 May. Available at http://www.highbeam.com/doc/1P2-20213025.html

Sadowski, Emma (2009) 'Eight more U.K. top 30 firms size up legal outsourcing moves'. *Legal Week*, 19 November. Available at http://www.legalweek.com/legal-week/news/1562452/eight-uk-firms-size-legal-outsourcing-moves

Sangani, Priyanka (2009) 'GE plans to turn India gradually into a sourcing base'. *The Economic Times*, 2 October. Available at http://articles.economictimes.indiatimes.com/2009-10-02/news/28380487_1_ge-india-ge-plans-tejpreet-chopra

Sengupta, Sniqdha (2008) 'We play in uncontested spaces: Raman Roy'. *StartupCentral*, 5 July. Available at http://startupcentral.in/2008/07/raman-roy-on-babel-and-more/

SDD Global (2009) Company information available at http://www.sddglobal.com

Shivkamal (2008) 'Big Blue blossoms in India'. *IBEF MNC Watch*, 21 April. Available at www.ibef.org/download/MNC_WATCH_042108.pdf

Singh, Shelley (2007) 'Quatrro BPO buys out eIndia's stake'. *The Economic Times*, 20 April. Available at http://articles.economictimes.indiatimes.com/2007-04-20/news/28474271_1_flextronics-bpo-roy-s-quatrro-bpo-solutions-kpo

Singh, Shelley and Shubham Mukherjee (2008) 'The Raman Effect'. *The Economic Times*, 19 April. Available at http://economictimes.indiatimes.com/Features/Special_Pages/The_Leisure_Lounge/The_Raman_effect/articleshow/msid-2963138,curpg-1.cms

Srikanth, R. P. (2002) 'Indian BPO players wear value-added services hat'. *Express Computer*, 29 July. Available at http://www.expresscomputeronline.com/20020729/cover.shtml

Srivastava, Mehul (2009) 'India: Worries grow about Obama outsourcing policies'. *Bloomberg Businessweek*, 3 March. Available at http://www.businessweek.com/globalbiz/content/mar2009/gb2009033_652807.htm

Srivastava, Prasoon (2009) 'India to add more rules in IT act soon'. *CIOL News*, 1 October. Available at http://www.ciol.com/News/News-Reports/India-to-add-more-rules-in-IT-Act-soon/11009125822/0/

Solomon, Jay and Kathryn Kranhold (2005) 'In India's outsourcing boom, GE played a starring role'. *The Wall Street Journal*, 23 March. Available at http://www.cwalocal4250.org/outsourcing/binarydata/GE%20Role.pdf

Souza, Val (2008) 'Sustaining India's software services success story'. *CSI Newstrac*. Available at http://www.thefreelibrary.com/Sustaining+India's+Software+Services+Success+Story-a01073895661

Symphony (2009) Unless otherwise stated all quotes are taken from interviews with Symphony top management or from internal company documents.

Thayer, Ann M. (2009) 'From compound to pill'. *Chemical & Engineering News*, 19 January. Available at http://pubs.acs.org/cen/coverstory/87/8703cover2.html

The Economic Times (3 July 2003) 'B'lore research makes GE wash more efficiently'. Available at http://articles.economictimes.indiatimes.com/2003-07-03/news/27555273_1_jfwtc-power-systems-medical-systems

The Economic Times (4 March 2009) 'IT exports to touch $62 bn by FY 2011'. Available at http://articles.economictimes.indiatimes.com/2009-03-04/news/28409422_1_bpo-export-indian-it-bpo-industry-exports-sector

The Economic Times (6 June 2006) 'Raman Roy's Quatrro to buy FSS BPO'. Available at http://articles.economictimes.indiatimes.com/2006-06-06/news/27461732_1_raman-roy-s-quatrro-anik-technologies-john-keells

The Economic Times (2 July 2008) 'Quatrro buys UK gaming co Babel Media'. Available at http://articles.economictimes.indiatimes.com/2008-07-02/news/27711198_1_quatrro-bpo-majority-stake-olympus-capital

The Economic Times (2 August 2009) '$70 bn drugs to go off-patent, benefiting India'. Available at http://articles.economictimes.indiatimes.com/2009-08-02/news/28385447_1_health-regulator-pharma-industry-approvals

The Economic Times (5 December 2008) 'Quatrro BPO may acquire about half-a-dozen cos'. Available at http://articles.economictimes.indiatimes.com/2008-12-05/news/28472593_1_quatrro-bpo-solutions-majority-stake-olympus-capital

The Financial Express (14 May 2007) 'The new outsourcing pill'. Available at http://www.financialexpress.com/news/The-new-outsourcing-pill/166308/

The Financial Express (22 May 2009) 'Dr Reddy's shuts R&D centre at Atlanta'. Available at http://www.financialexpress.com/news/dr-reddys-shuts-r&d-centre-at-atlanta/463916/0

The Hindu Business Line (3 June 2006) 'IBM Daksh expands employee base'. Available at http://www.thehindubusinessline.in/2006/06/03/stories/2006060300610400.htm

The Hindu Business Line (30 September 2008) 'Pharma outsourcing industry to cross $2.5 bn by 2012: Zinnov'. Available at http://www.zinnov.com/press.php?pr_id=57&PHPSESSID=9eaebf760fd2bf1ddae5b87118b73e68

The Times of India (11 November 2009) 'Director of BPO unit held for data theft'. Available at http://articles.timesofindia.indiatimes.com/2009-11-11/pune/28079904_1_bpo-unit-data-theft-cyber-cell

Thimmaya, P. P. (2009) 'Genpact eyes 15% revenue growth', *The Economic Times*, 22 May. Available at http://articles.economictimes.indiatimes.com/2009-05-22/news/27657501_1_genpact-eyes-outsourcing-contracts-revenue

ValueNotes (November 2009) 'Legal Process Outsourcing: Crisis Creates New Opportunities for LPOs'. Available at http://www.sourcingnotes.com/content/view/554/1/

Wilson, Ron (2008) 'FPGAs aren't gone yet – or even slowing down. But ...'. *EDN*, 12 August. Available at http://www.edn com/blog/Practical_Chip_Design/37834-FPGAs_aren_t_gone_yet_or_even_slowing_down_But_.php

Zinnov (June 2009) 'India R&D: Vision 2019'. Available at http://www.zinnov.com/pdfFiles/1254815402orv_India_RD_Vision_2019.ppt__Compatibility_Mode_.pdf

Index